PENGUIN

THE ART OF FOCUS

Gauranga Das is a leadership and mindfulness coach based in Mumbai. A graduate from IIT Bombay, he found his calling to become a monk. A member of the Governing Body Commission at International Society for Krishna Consciousness (ISKCON), he is actively involved in enhancing leadership effectiveness and governance of temples and communities globally. He is dedicated to helping people transform their hearts, establish sustainable and spiritual communities, and drive a positive change in society. A multifaceted spiritualist on a mission to create a value-based society, he is a mindful meditation expert, strategic character educationist, sustainability and climate change warrior, and social welfare catalyst.

He is the director of ISKCON's Govardhan Ecovillage (GEV), founded by Radhanath Swami. The GEV, representing India, has won over thirty-six national and international awards, including the UN World Tourism Organization (UNWTO) Award in 2017 for its innovative model of 'Eco-Tourism as a Catalyst for Rural Development'. Gauranga Das has also strategized and led the execution of GEV's synergistic solution for Sustainable Development Goals (SDGs) for climate change and enabled GEV's accreditation to multiple UN bodies such as UNEP, UN ECOSOC, UNCCD and UNCBD. He is the UNEP's Faith for Earth counsellor on behalf of ISKCON. The Indian Green Building Council (IGBC) has recognized him as an IGBC fellow for his contribution to the green building movement.

He sits on the board of the Govardhan School of Public Leadership, an institution that prepares students for the civil services exam. He has led several youth empowerment initiatives across the world to successfully inculcate in them clarity in purpose, purity in character and compassion in relationships. He is also the administrative director of the Bhaktivedanta Research Center (BRC), an initiative of ISKCON to connect professionals, housewives and students to the academic study of philosophy, create libraries of Vedic literatures and manuscripts, and facilitate MA and PhD programmes in philosophy.

ALSO BY THE SAME AUTHOR

The Art of Resilience

ADVANCE PRAISE FOR THE BOOK

'In this age of Internet and social media, focus is a precious commodity to possess. People who can get away from the clutter of the mind and can focus on their priorities will be the ones to succeed in life. I am sure that *The Art of Focus* will help all its readers to move towards that goal'—Bhagat Singh Koshyari, governor of Maharashtra

'*Dharmo Rakshati Rakshitah* means that dharma protects us if we follow [respect] it. Dharma, "the law" that maintains the equilibrium of the universe, also provides the principles for a fulfilling and purpose-driven life. In *The Art of Focus*, Swami ji has brought out these principles of dharma in a very simple way—in the form of simple, everyday stories and anecdotes—that drive home the point and keep us "focused" to follow our dharma to achieve health, happiness and harmony in life' —Arun Kankani, president, Sewa International Inc, USA

'In this era of digital, technology has become truly pervasive. *The Art of Focus* masterfully guides the reader to cultivate a focused mind and take charge of their digital lives'—Aarthi Subramanian, group chief digital officer, Tata Sons

'Today, we oftentimes go out to help others when, before that, we ourselves need help. *The Art of Focus* takes the reader on an inward journey to find the deeper meaning of life within the core of the heart, while intertwining its essence with the difference one can make in the world outside'—Aditya Natraj, CEO, Piramal Foundation

'In recent years, there has been a lot of talk around mental health globally. *The Art of Focus* not just enlightens [us] on this but actually transcends to focus on spiritual health. What makes the presentation unique is its simplicity'—Sangita Reddy, joint managing director, Apollo Hospitals Group

'Discipline steers constant growth and development. Gauranga Das beautifully narrates how focus is actually the starting point of it all and how the journey to spiritual evolution begins here. One couldn't begin 2022 more positively than by reading this bundle of wisdom'—

Kiran Bedi, twenty-fourth lieutenant governor of Puducherry, and founder, India Vision Foundation and Navjyoti India Foundation

'The world we live in has come a long way in recent decades. While the wants have multiplied, the needs have remained the same. A core need of the soul is to feel love and share love. In *The Art of Focus*, Gauranga Das presents ways in which we can pursue this gradually and sustainably. To me, what stood out is the variety in stories and depth in analysis'—Rajashree Birla, chairperson, Aditya Birla Centre for Community Initiative and Rural Development

THE art OF FOCUS

45 STORIES *to* uplift the mind
and transform the heart

GAURANGA DAS

PENGUIN
ANANDA

An imprint of Penguin Random House

PENGUIN ANANDA

USA | Canada | UK | Ireland | Australia
New Zealand | India | South Africa | China

Penguin Ananda is part of the Penguin Random House group of companies
whose addresses can be found at global.penguinrandomhouse.com

Published by Penguin Random House India Pvt. Ltd
4th Floor, Capital Tower 1, MG Road,
Gurugram 122 002, Haryana, India

Penguin
Random House
India

First published in Penguin Ananda by Penguin Random House India 2022

ISBN 9780143452744

Typeset in Adobe Caslon Pro by MAP Systems, Bangalore, India

All proceeds from the sale of this book will be directly utilized
for the Govardhan Annakshetra food distribution programme.

www.penguin.co.in

To the three people who changed my life forever—
His Divine Grace A.C. Bhaktivedanta Swami Srila Prabhupada,
the founder Acharya of ISKCON;
His Holiness Radhanath Swami, my spiritual master;
and His Holiness Bhakti Rasamrita Swami,
my first spiritual mentor.

Contents

Introduction

I have been a monk for over thirty years. When I tell people I am a monk, the image they seem to conjure up is that of a man of the cloth who meditates in tranquillity for hours on end. In part, they are correct. I do mediate for over two hours daily, chanting the Hare Krishna mantra with focused attention. However, the other twenty-two hours are filled with a different flavour of tranquillity. They are filled with being involved in a plethora of selfless services that are spiritually inspired.

For one of these services, I travel the world speaking about the Vedic literatures I have studied intensively and based my life on. Specifically, the three main literatures, including the famous *Bhagavad Gita As It Is*, heralded as the main source of wisdom for Hindus globally and from which most lessons of these books are derived. It is sometimes cited as the textbook of God. The second book is the *Srimad Bhagavatam*, an extensive 18,000-verse treatise on God by Veda Vyasa, translated into English by A.C. Bhaktivedanta Swami Srila Prabhupada. This book is sometimes cited as the biography of God. The third book is the *Chaitanya Charitamrita*, the life and teachings of Sri Chaitanya Mahaprabhu, a fifteenth-century incarnation of God. This book is sometimes cited as the diary of God. Each book has its place in society; each adding layers of truths about the Supreme, just as a child is taught about the rules of mathematics as they advance from one grade to another.

From my experience speaking around the world, I have realized that for many it is easier to absorb the truths of literatures like the *Bhagavad Gita As It Is* when it is supplemented by stories. Stories give a context and application to truth. Stories help us imagine ourselves in the characters' roles and apply the lesson that they are learning into our own lives. It is easier to learn the lesson of 'being grateful' in the context of a story rather than be told to simply 'be grateful'. There is no doubt about the appeal of ancient Vedic heavyweight literatures such as the Mahabharata and the Ramayana. They are so popular because they teach universal truths through stories unparalleled in their excitement, engagement and depth.

The Art of Focus is the second book in the three-part series. It takes the same principle of telling enamouring cultural stories and bringing to light universal truths that are found within them. As stated, I have primarily used the *Bhagavad Gita As It Is* to bring out the lessons of these stories. The main topics include understanding the spiritual nature of the human condition (*atma*), the components of the world around us (*prakriti*), the influence time has on our life (*kala*), how our actions in the past created our present and how our present actions can affect our future (*karma*) and the influence of the Supreme control over everything and everyone (*isvara*).

This book is for those keen to build focus, as we live in a world replete with distractions. Distractions, not just in the form of electronic gadgets but in the variety of entertainment and the plethora of lifestyle options available in the modern age. Hence, it's not surprising that a recent research reported that the human attention span is less than that of a goldfish (at nine seconds). Building focus is the first step to leading a life based on purpose. Focus helps build discipline, willpower and persistence to pursue our goals consistently and accomplish life's mission assiduously. The COVID-19 pandemic has transformed the way we look at life and how we prioritize the various aspects of life. As the world recoups and gathers strength after experiencing multiple waves of the pandemic, building focus is a prerequisite to staying the course in our life's journey to pursue eco-friendly growth and development while maintaining holistic well-being (physical, mental and spiritual).

What makes this book different is that the everlasting principles explaining the stories are based on authentic, timeless Vedic wisdom. They address issues at a level far beyond the popular and well-trodden path of self-help. These principles are also eternal and time-tested, and can enrich our lives if we follow them sincerely. I do not claim to be the author of these ideas. Indeed, these ideas originate in Krishna Himself and have been taught by several spiritual teachers like His Divine Grace (H.D.G.) Srila A.C. Bhaktivedanta Swami Prabhupada, the Founder Acharya of the International Society of Krishna Consciousness (ISKCON), to those committed to understanding Him in succession. I am simply an instrument to help you find relevance, utility and joyful transformation through these topics and do my utmost to show you how they can be applied to the real world.

ONE

In It Together

Human Quality: Association

Harish was a trained software engineer who worked with a leading IT product multinational company in Bangalore. He lived in a plush villa nestled between two lakes and surrounded by greenery. He was an avid spiritual seeker and part of a group that got together to discuss spiritual topics under a mentor. Harish, who used to be an active participant in the group meetings, had recently stopped participating in them without notice. After a few weeks on one very cold night, Mohan, the leader of the group, decided to visit Harish. Mohan found Harish at home, alone, seated in front of the fireplace, where a bright fire burned.

Initially reluctant, but out of regard, Harish walked up to the door and welcomed Mohan inside. They smiled at each other and exchanged pleasantries. There was a loud silence for a while. The sound of singing insects like cicadas, crickets, grasshoppers and katydids filled the atmosphere, adding to the feelings of discomfort in Harish. Mohan was in two minds whether to moot a conversation or wait for Harish to initiate it. The two men watched the dancing flames around the logs.

The flames crackled in the fireplace. The silence continued for a few more minutes.

Then, Mohan, without saying a word, diverted Harish's attention. He stood up, examined the logs under the fire and with a pair of tongs, latched on to one that glowed the brightest of all. He removed it from the fire and kept it aside. Smiling at Harish, Mohan returned to his seat.

Harish was paying attention to Mohan's actions and was keen to know why he did what he did and what was going to happen next. Before long, the flame on the lone log subsided, until there was only a momentary glow. Shortly, the fire went out.

Within minutes, what was previously bright, lit and radiating heat became nothing more than a black and dead piece of wood. The eerie silence continued as they saw the dead piece of wood remain isolated from the bright fire radiating heat and providing warmth on that cold night. The gentlemen continued to look at the flames and the isolated log alternately.

In a while, Mohan got up. With the tongs in his right hand, he picked up the isolated piece of wood, apparently of no use, and placed it right back where it was—in the middle of the fire. Right away, it rekindled, fuelled by the light and heat of the burning logs around. In deep thought, Harish looked at Mohan. They smiled at each other. Not a single word was exchanged.

As Mohan began to walk to the door, Harish joined him. As they reached the door, Harish tapped on Mohan's shoulder and said, 'Thank you for your visit. More importantly, thank you for your beautiful lesson. I'll return to the group soon.'

With a smile, Mohan hugged him and said, 'Thank you. See you soon.'

The host bid goodbye to the leader and returned to the fireplace, feeling relieved and comforted by the leader's inspiration.

Let's understand the importance of association or being in a group of good people or sadhu sanga.

In his essay titled 'A Deliberation on the Methodology of Sadhu-sanga', the great Vaishnava reformer, Bhaktivinoda Thakura, wrote, 'The quartz crystal assumes the colour of any object in its proximity, regardless of the hue of that object.'

It's important to choose the people we associate with. There are two criteria suggested: values and gravitas.

The first quality you want to look for is values. The values that they uphold should be those of morality and divinity. We should seek people whose values resonate with ours accordingly. The second criterion, gravitas, refers to having greater skill, cognitive ability, experience or talent in areas that we are working on. This could be behavioural or technical. Not only are they better in this area, but they're also confident enough to not tear you down to make themselves look better or even feel better. Choosing such people will inspire you in the journey of self-discovery. It's important to realize that being the 'smartest' person in the room is gratifying to the ego, but it's not conducive to our personal and professional growth.

The great acharya of the Bhakti movement, Srila Narottama Dāsa Ṭhākura, lamented in his song, 'Gora Pahun' or 'Aksepa', that when one deviates from pure consciousness of Kṛṣṇa, one becomes entangled in material activities.

sat-sanga chāḍi' kainu asate vilāsa
te-kāraṇe lāgilo ye karma-bandha-phānsa

Avoiding the association of saintly persons, I sported merrily in the company of materialistic rascals. For that reason, I have become strung up in the noose of my own fruitive activities.

Let's look at the flip side of bad associations and what we should avoid. Here is a lesson from the Mahabharata. Dhritarashtra, because of his attachment to Duryodhana and that association, acted in the most abominable and sinful way, and all of his spiritual principles were compromised. No matter how great you are, if you choose bad associates, you will become abominable in the eyes of God. Who are we in comparison to Dhritarashtra? Sometimes, we think that Dhritarashtra was such an evil man but actually he was a descendant of the Kuru dynasty, the eldest of three brothers and factually the son of Veda Vyas, which means he was directly the son of the literary incarnation of God, and what is the type of high birth we have? And Dhritarashtra was spoon-fed and trained by Bhishma himself. Dhritarashtra had the best birth from the best family; he was trained by a legendary teacher. He had only one defect: he was attached to the association of somebody who was very greedy for power and could not control his mind and senses.

Going back to the story and the analogy of the logs elicited by the leader, each member in the group helps the other. There is a positive give and take, one that helps each one in the group make progress. Just as the logs of wood take fire and heat from the rest while making their own contribution, it's worth reminding the group members that they are a part of the flame. It's key to recall that in unison we are all responsible for keeping each other's flame burning. More than that, to sustain the fire for a long period, we must promote union among a favourable group so that the fire is really strong, effective and lasting.

A group is also a family. There are times when incidents cause us to drift apart, but we need to look at why we came together, the higher purpose. It doesn't matter if we are, at times, bothered by unfortunate quarrels and misunderstandings. What matters is that we remain connected. Let's focus on learning and drawing inspiration from one another to keep the flame burning bright.

TWO

The Battle of Insects

Human Quality: Mindfulness

It was the month of March in the nineteenth century in the scenic city of Colorado, well known for its vivid landscape of mountains, forests, high plains, mesas, canyons, plateaus, rivers and desert lands. Colorado is one of the mountain states and a part of the western and south-western US.

John and his father, Philip, walked through the woods on a pleasant Saturday morning in March. February is the start of the warmer months of spring, followed by the summer months in Colorado. This is also that time of the year when, as the temperature goes up, tree sap flows down while leaves and fruits are in full bloom. A high schooler, John was in deep thought about charting the course for the next phase of his life. He wanted to discuss certain ideas he had in mind and hoped that his father would guide and give him direction.

As John looked ahead, he slowed down. He was captivated by the sight of a tree. Sensing that John was a few steps behind him, Philip asked, 'What happened, John?'

'Dad, what tree is that?' asked John, while in deep thought, pointing to a tall tree that had fallen on the ground just a few metres ahead.

'Well, that's a birch tree,' Philip affirmed.

'I see,' said John.

'About 70 feet tall, the birch is a thin-leaved deciduous hardwood tree. Did you know that the history of this species of trees is interesting?'

'Is it?' John was curious. 'Tell me more . . .'

Philip stopped walking and stood right next to the long bark of the fallen tree. In a deep voice, Philip went on, 'This tree that you see survives storms, avalanches and various kinds of natural cataclysmic events for over hundred years. That tree may have been around when American independence was won in 1776.'

'Interesting . . .' John remarked.

'Despite the many storms and other upheavals,' Philip continued, 'the tree survives. But do you know what probably brought it down?'

'What?' asked John, 'Maybe it lost its strength and became weak?.

'Not really,' his father smiled. 'What finally brought the tree down was not an avalanche, or a massive thunderstorm, or a tornado or even a cyclone. The tree was ultimately attacked by insects, which started eating the bark of the tree from within.'

'What!' John was amazed. 'How is that possible?'

'Yes, it is possible and that's what makes the history of this tree interesting and something for us to learn,' Philip narrated. 'Gradually, the insects entered the trunk. As the insects started eating the tree from within, that tree, which stood strong against all kinds of attacks of nature, ultimately collapsed and fell to the ground.'

'Wow! How tragic!'

'Yes, wood-boring insects are among the most destructive pests when it comes to ornamental trees and shrubs. Most of these insects are the larvae of certain moths and beetles. They tunnel and feed under the bark in living wood, destroying water- and sap-conducting tissues. This causes girdling, branch dieback, structural weakness, decline and eventual death of susceptible plants.'

'I never knew about this,' John replied. 'This is indeed a powerful story.'

'The truth is,' Philip went on, 'even today, anyone can go and see the ruins of such species of trees in Colorado. This serves as testimony that it is not always the large external attacks that cause one's downfall. Often, what we consider puny or very insignificant can destroy us from within.'

'Indeed, dad,' John admitted. 'We often tend to look outside and not within.'

'That's right, John,' Philip tapped John on the shoulder. 'But when we ignore them and when we do not overpower them, we allow them to constantly attack us from within, unaware of the perils surrounding us.'

'So true, dad. Dangerously similar to this tree, we get consumed by those infesting us from within.'

'Well said, John.'

'Thank you, dad, for sharing this valuable lesson.'

Philip tapped his son on the shoulder. Inspired by this story, John felt comfortable enough to open up and share with his father all that was playing on his mind. Then, they continued with their morning walk in the woods.

We experience problems in life, similar to tornadoes, cyclones, storms and tsunamis, such as poverty, infamy, attack on our character, various kinds of other physical attacks, attacks on our business or a much larger economic crisis affecting the world. We may bring all of our energy together and fight back but it is not usually these huge calamities that cause our downfall, as we saw in the case of the birch tree. There are dangerous elements like lust, anger, greed, envy and illusion within us that cause our downfall and eat us from within.

Let's start with envy. Just like an insect, it is difficult to spot. Just the way an insect creates a hole within the tree and makes the trunk of the tree hollow, a similar situation can arise with envy. This emotion comes to the fore on occasions when there are sentiments in the heart related to envy of another's good fortune, being disturbed at seeing the wealth of others, displeasure and jealousy, etc. One of the greatest problems of a materialistic society is the tendency to compare yourself with others: 'I'm not as successful as this other person', 'I'm not as attractive as that other person', 'On social media, this person has so many more likes than I do', 'I need a better car than my neighbour', 'I need to go on better vacations than my colleague', etc. However, comparing yourself with others is bound to lead to the impression that you are a failure because there is always someone who is more successful, intelligent and interesting than you.

The moment we start comparing ourselves with others, we enter the land of frustration. The mentality of comparison breeds the greatest obstacle for spiritual life: envy. Envy is the opponent of love. In fact, envy arises when we find something better in others. Rather, with a gracious heart, we should appreciate and express love for others.

Krishna describes in the Bhagavad Gita (2.62),

> *dhyāyato viṣayān puṁsaḥ*
> *saṅgas teṣūpajāyate*
> *saṅgāt sañjāyate kāmaḥ*
> *kāmāt krodho 'bhijāyate*

While contemplating the objects of the senses, a person develops an attachment for them and from such attachment, lust develops and from lust anger arises.

Desires, when unfulfilled, lead to anger. Desires, when fulfilled, may satisfy us for some time but then our desire increases, leading to greed and ultimately dissatisfaction.

The Bhagavad Gita explains (3.39),

> *āvṛtaṁ jñānam etena*
> *jñānino nitya-vairiṇā*
> *kāma-rūpeṇa kaunteya*
> *duṣpūreṇānalena ca*

Thus the wise living entity's pure consciousness becomes covered by his eternal enemy in the form of lust, which is never satisfied and which burns like fire.

The Bhagavad Gita adds (2.63):

krodhād bhavati sammohaḥ
sammohāt smṛti-vibhramaḥ
smṛti-bhraṁśād buddhi-nāśo
buddhi-nāśāt praṇaśyati

From anger arises complete delusion and from delusion, bewilderment of memory. When memory is bewildered, intelligence is lost. When intelligence is lost, one falls down once again into the materialistic pool.

According to Ayurveda, lust (kama), anger (krodha) and greed (lobha) are the three main causes for almost all diseases. Kama and krodha last only for a few minutes and have a time limit. However, lobha has no limit. It's a monster that can eat one from within.

It's important that we do not underestimate the various insidious feelings that arise from within the heart or think that they are insignificant—just like the insects appeared insignificant in the story. They, in fact, had the capacity to create a cavity within a gigantic tree, leaving it in ruins. Drawing inspiration from this lesson, let's not allow insects like lust, anger, greed, illusion and envy to eat us from within and wreak havoc in our lives. Rather, let's develop positive feelings of love, appreciation and contentment in life.

THREE

The Memory of Love

Human Quality: Relationships

It was a dark evening during the monsoon season. That year, it was pouring more than usual, and the rain was accompanied by thunder and lightning. The air had become chilly as a result.

Seated in the lounge of Dr Kulkarni's clinic was Rajeev, an old man who was waiting for his turn to meet the doctor for a routine check-up after an injury. He usually visited in the forenoon. However, due to the non-stop downpour during the day, he couldn't step out earlier that day. He waited patiently for his turn. As soon as it was his turn, Rajeev entered the consulting room.

The doctor greeted Rajeev, who reciprocated very kindly with gratitude for Dr Kulkarni's medical help.

As was his usual practice, Dr Kulkarni started checking the stitches. As he was looking around, Rajeev noticed that it was 7.30 p.m.

Immediately, he requested Dr Kulkarni, 'Doctor, could you please finish these stitches quickly? I have to reach home within half hour.'

'Sure, Rajeev,' the doctor replied. 'I'll do my best.'

Incidentally, the rain had stopped. Rajeev was hoping that he could just leave and reach home on time. Despite the doctor's best efforts that day, he spotted a blood clot in the infected area and had to do more than usual to treat it. There was a delay and the treatment went on for a while.

The clock showed that it was 8 p.m. Rajeev noticed the time but remained silent, controlling the urge to leave. He understood the situation and recognized that the doctor was indeed busy at work.

Fifteen more minutes passed and it started to rain again.

Dr Kulkarni completed his work on the stitches. He apologized profusely, 'I'm sorry, Rajeev. You wanted to be home soon but somehow I could not finish examining you on time. Meanwhile, it is pouring as well. Forgive me.'

'That's okay, doctor,' Rajeev replied politely, looking at the rain through the window.

'If I may ask,' Dr Kulkarni continued, inquisitive, 'why are you in such a hurry to reach home? Is there a family get-together of sorts?'

With a wry smile, Rajeev replied, 'Actually, my wife is sick. She's suffering from Alzheimer's.'

The doctor's face turned pale, 'I'm sorry.'

Rajeev continued, 'Every day, I go there and spend time with her and she expects me to do so. But ultimately, she cannot remember who I am. But I still spend time with her.'

Those words left Dr Kulkarni bewildered. He looked at Rajeev in wonder, 'But if she doesn't remember who you are, why do you spend time with her? It doesn't make a difference whether you do or don't because she won't remember anyway.'

Rajeev nodded with a warm smile and added, 'That's true; she doesn't even remember whether I came to see her the previous day or not. But she gets happy when she sees me. She smiles.'

Dr Kulkarni added, 'But you said that she has no memory of you and doesn't even recognize you as her husband. Is it not strange that she cannot reciprocate or express her feelings for you?'

'That's right, doctor,' Rajeev replied, the pain obvious in his voice.

The doctor asked him politely, 'But then, Rajeev, why do you want to go? What do you get out of it?'

Rajeev remained silent for a few seconds. After deep thought and after clearing his throat, he said, 'Doctor, it is true that she does not know who I am. But I know who she is.'

Dr Kulkarni was moved by his statement.

Rajeev continued, '. . . therefore, it is my duty to express my gratitude, affection and reciprocation for all that she did for me and in memory of the times that we spent together. Yes, Alzheimer's has taken away her memory but it has not taken away my memory.'

Inspired by Rajeev's affection for his wife, Dr Kulkarni hugged him and bid him goodbye. Having expressed his heart thoroughly, Rajeev felt good inside. Just as Rajeev started leaving and looking at the heavy downpour, Dr Kulkarni asked him to wait and requested his driver to drop him home.

This story of Rajeev's attitude towards his wife tells us about the natural result of pure love. Love is unconditional and requires sincerity from our heart to express it and make the other person feel special despite the challenges that we face or the apparent shortcomings that we see in the other person. In relationships, there are always impediments and personal inconveniences that can occur. However, we should take care to not let that interfere with our love. And under all circumstances, we should strive to serve our beloved and show love.

Often times, we wonder how love can blossom between people at all times—despite challenging situations and even if these situations don't alter significantly, when there is inherent diversity in personality with differing likes and dislikes, varying capabilities, areas of interests, etc. Besides, we as people change with time and so do our expectations from life, self and the people around us. This is restricted not just to relationships between partners but even between friends. Often, we see people who were thick as thieves in school or college disconnect many years down the line. We have seen this between partners as well. We have all witnessed one partner stating that he/she can no longer feel the spark of love that existed at the start of the relationship or courtship.

The following principles can help improve relationships by encouraging diversity and natural growth, thus facilitating fulfillment:

- **Engage People According To Their Propensities:** Even at the start of a relationship, between the sparks that fly (as they say) and the involuntary attraction that follows, it's important to keenly understand and observe what drives the other person from within or what his/her propensities are. That's a key determinant of the longevity and stability of a relationship. By propensity, I mean the natural inclination that someone has towards something and that which largely shapes their purpose in life. For example, someone could have a propensity for social work or pursuit of an art form professionally or spirituality or entrepreneurship or serving the military, etc. These are examples at the macro level. At a micro level, there could be hobbies and interests that shape people's leisure time. These could be gardening, listening to music, teaching the underprivileged, playing an instrument, etc. After the early years in a relationship, supporting each other in these aspects will go a long way in taking the relationship forward.

- **Recognize Multiple Ways of Getting Things Done Effectively:** Based on the personality that people have, there are ways in which we do things. Before we get to the action part or to how people do it, it's important to understand the 'why' part of it—what motivates/drives an action. One set of people could be task-based, while the other could be feelings-based. The former is not emotional but is keen on completion of a task on time. However, the latter is receptive to people's feelings, sometimes sentimental too, such that they prioritize the feelings and comfort of the people they work with and completion of tasks take a backseat. This is one pair with differing personality types. Another example is that of a perfectionist who would want to complete one task before moving on to the next even if he/she is required to wait to complete the first task. However, a multitasker would be able to juggle both tasks together. So, there is no one right way of doing things. It's always about understanding and acknowledging the differences in each other's personality, embracing diversity to learn from each other, adjusting at most times and complementing each other in the way we organize our life to leverage the strengths in our partner's personality.

- **Recognize People's Right and Need for Independent Thinking:** While a relationship is about sharing life, give and take, and supporting each other through thick and thin, it's important to understand that we are fundamentally jīva (the soul) clad in a temporary body. At the core, the soul is independent and has its own propensities. Hence, it's important to recognize that vital aspect and give space to people in a relationship. Maintaining this balance of sharing and giving space is crucial.

FOUR

Talking Frog and Determination

Human Quality: Focus

Shweta, a teenager, was walking on the road on a fine monsoon morning in the scenic town of Kasauli in Himachal Pradesh. It had rained heavily over the past couple of days. That morning, the sun arrived, giving much-needed cheer to the people. Gradually, the people made their way out of their homes for their daily chores.

Shweta was on her way to purchase groceries for her mother so she could prepare breakfast. Suddenly, Shweta spotted a golden frog next to some trees. Amazingly, the frog jumped into the middle of the road and started speaking to her.

In a deep voice, it croaked, 'If you hold me and follow my instructions, I will turn into a handsome prince.' An amused Shweta immediately picked up the frog, put it in her handbag and kept walking.

Baffled by her indifferent response, the golden frog demanded an immediate audience with Shweta. As she opened her handbag, the frog looked at her and proposed, 'If you lift me up and scratch under my neck, I will turn into a handsome prince.' Again, Shweta did not show much excitement over its offer. She stayed mum and kept walking.

Flustered by her placid response, the frog croaked and then jumped on to her arm to demand her attention. The shrill noise made by the frog could have provoked a normal person but Shweta kept walking without paying attention to the frog.

Rattled by Shweta's equanimity, the frog squealed, 'I was a charming prince but now I'm caught in a frog's body. So, lift me up, scratch under my neck and see what happens. What have you got to lose?'

Smiling gently, she affirmed, 'Well, I'm a student and I'd rather work hard today to build my future tomorrow.' She continued in an assertive tone, 'I do not have time for any prince charming or anyone else for that matter.'

With a smile, she gently tapped the frog on its head and remarked: 'A talking frog though, that's pretty cool to have!' With these words, she continued to walk on the road.

Have we not experienced such situations in life quite often?

As we walk on our path in life, as a student, as an employee or as a family member, we undertake various responsibilities and perform many duties. Each path is riddled with obvious distractions, enticing invitations and attractive escape routes. How can we avoid getting distracted by the many alternatives that the mind and the world present us with? Only by living a purpose-driven life. Those who commit to nothing are distracted by everything.

Shri Krishna recommends in the Bhagavad Gita (2.41):

> *vyavasāyātmikā buddhir*
> *ekeha kuru-nandana*
> *bahu-śākhā hy anantāś ca*
> *buddhayo 'vyavasāyinām*

Without sustained determination, we cannot expect to achieve much in life. While others can guide, inspire or even prod us, the journey to achieving a goal is to be undertaken by us personally. And how do we cultivate sustained determination? The Gita's recommendation is by putting purpose ahead of pleasure.

Now, how do we put purpose ahead of pleasure at all times? For that, let's dwell on thoughts that drive us to act. Throughout the day, no matter whether we are at work or at leisure or munching something, we think about something or the other. Thoughts are very important in that they, in a way, define our personality. Thoughts that sprout in the mind eventually mushroom into words that we speak or spur us into actions that we perform.

So, it's important that we understand the nature of thoughts. They fall into four categories:

- **Necessary:** These are related to our day-to-day activities. These can involve something as basic as the thought of brushing our teeth right after waking up to purchasing groceries to responding to an official email (in case of professionals) or studying for an upcoming exam (in case of students). These are important thoughts to have as they help us regularize our daily activities and inculcate discipline in us and help us lead an orderly life.
- **Positive:** These are value-based thoughts and have the power to infuse in us positive energy. These thoughts include the urge from within to show compassion, the eagerness to express appreciation, the earnestness to seek forgiveness, the sincerity to show respect to elders, etc.

The energy that is generated as a result of these thoughts affects our mind positively and makes the heart feel lighter. These are thoughts with no selfish intentions.

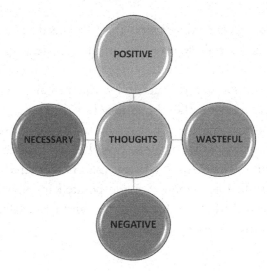

- **Wasteful:** The mind tends to brood over past incidents or worry about the future. As a result, this leads to thoughts of angst, regret, disappointment, worry, confusion, sense of fear, etc. Such thoughts do not allow us to perform to the best of our potential. Rather, they pull us away from even performing our duties and responsibilities.

- **Negative:** Based on our interactions and the different experiences we encounter in this world, the mind collects our responses (sometimes involuntary) to situations and there are tendencies to form what we refer to as our weaknesses, complexes, etc. Such thoughts are negative and should be avoided at all costs. These includes vices and evil thoughts as well like envy, jealousy, pride, anger, lust, etc. Ayurvedic studies say that such negative thoughts produce toxins in the body, which are detrimental to our well-being.

For us to become distraction-free, we need to maximize positive and necessary thoughts and minimize negative and wasteful thoughts.

Let us not get distracted by the promises of short-lived pleasures, whether by aimlessly surfing the Internet, whiling away time on social media or wastefully spending precious time in other aimless ways. Let us value the gift of opportunities that God has given us. The cluttered mind is best controlled by applying single-pointed intelligence to a goal. Our real friend is determination and not a talking frog with princely promises.

FIVE

Whose Compassion Is Higher?

Human Quality: Compassion

While on the shore of the Ganga, a disciple earnestly asked his guru, 'Master, please can you explain to me what is compassion?'

The sage, while waiting for a ferryboat, looked around and drew his inquisitive student's attention to a figure at a distance. 'Do you see that beggar there?'

The sincere student responded by respectfully nodding yes.

'Observe the beggar carefully,' the guru added.

As the student keenly observed, he noticed an affluent woman pass by. She looked at the poor beggar and gave him a gold coin.

As the disciple kept looking, a little while later, a wealthy merchant passed the beggar. He got off his horse cart and acknowledged the greetings of the people in the vicinity. Much to the delight of the beggar, the merchant gave him five gold coins, dropping them one after another into his bowl. With a wide smile on his face, the merchant got back into the cart and moved along.

Shortly thereafter, an innocent boy with a bag hanging over his right shoulder passed by the debilitated beggar. With flowers in his hand, the boy was walking exuberantly. As he chanced upon the beggar, the boy smiled at him, pulled his hand out and handed him some of the flowers.

Feeling good, the student turned to his master. Then, as they both looked at the river, they saw a pleasant sight of birds flying together in circles and soaring higher in the sky. As they flew higher, they made a sweet sound.

Now, to answer his student's question, the guru asked his student: 'My dear student, you saw three people help the beggar. Whose contribution do you think was the highest?'

The student gave the obvious response, 'The merchant gave the beggar five gold coins. That contribution was the highest.' The guru replied with a smile, 'Yes and no.'

Tightening his grip over his cane, the guru stood up and explained, 'When the woman saw the beggar's condition, she quietly handed him a gold coin out of pity over his condition. Next, as the merchant got off the horse cart, he was surrounded by many people who knew him. In order to display his wealth in front of them, out of pride he gave five gold coins while making sure that each coin made a loud clinging noise in the beggar's bowl. Contributions made as an expression of pride and pity are not the highest.'

The student nodded in anticipation of what his master was going to add.

The guru continued, 'Then that boy came by. If you noticed, he had a shopping bag hanging on his shoulder and he was carrying some flowers in his hands. Maybe, he was sent to purchase some groceries by his mother and he had picked some flowers for her, out of love, on the way back. Inspired by a similar feeling of love, as he saw the beggar's painful condition and spontaneously spared for him some of his 'wealth'—the flowers. That contribution was made out of pure, selfless compassion.'

The student bowed down in front of his master and gratefully accepted the message of love.

When fear touches pain, it is called pity. But when love touches pain, it is called compassion.

> *mānasa, deho, geho, jo kichu mor*
> *arpilū tuwā pade, nanda-kiśor!*
> *sampade vipade, jīvane-maraṇe*
> *dāy mama gelā, tuwā o-pada baraṇe*

The great Vaishnava reformer, Srila Bhaktivinoda Thakura, says here, 'My dear Lord, I offer to You my mind, my senses, my intelligence, my body and my entire existence. Because I see that when I serve You out of love, my heart is filled with attachment for You. As that attachment grows stronger, unselfish love overflows in my heart. This pure love for You converts into compassion for all living beings who are Your creation. Thus, my dear Lord, I engage all my assets for Your pleasure, in Your service.'

In the same mood as that of the poet, let us try to transform our heart with real love. In our daily lives, we are presented with moments when someone reaches out to us for help. Sometimes, we tend to act impulsively due to various reasons. It's good to take a deep breath and then tell yourself that this is an opportunity to show compassion and make a difference to their lives. Likewise, we find so many opportunities to show real compassion and thus transform the world by the power of such compassion.

Compassion is manifested by the following ingredients. If we can inculcate in us the following qualities, compassion will manifest on its own naturally:

- **Humility:** It means to think of oneself as insignificant. Now, we need not artificially act that way. It's important that we understand what humility is. Humility is honesty. To say that I'm poor when I'm rich or ugly when I'm beautiful is not humility, nor is admitting that I lack certain qualities when I possess them—that's just a statement of fact. Giving others credit and showing appreciation while minimizing our own accomplishments and capabilities, while on the inside we actually long for respect and recognition, is not humility. This false humility—while often a social necessity—is a lie. Part of real humility is accepting the whole truth: I have this possession or quality or ability by the grace of God. It's a gift given by God and the real understanding should be that if the assets are God's, then my pride should be for Him. I should be proud of His beauty or intelligence or wealth or talent, a part of which He is allowing me to exhibit on His behalf.

  Humility is also about being grateful, more than the understanding that everything belongs to God. It's important to realize that God has given us beauty or wealth or talent and has empowered us to live in a certain way and with certain riches. It's these qualities that help us in a way to earn a certain name in society and pursue a certain standard of life. It's said that gratitude is a great attitude.

Further, humility is also about being joyful. We remain joyful to express the gratitude that we have for what God has bestowed upon us. The joy is expressed with the mindset as God's child; that we do what will please Him.

- **Tolerance:** This is the second ingredient to build compassion. It means to be willing to endure difficulty and discomfort.

Krishna says in the Bhagavad Gita (2.14),

> *mātrā-sparśās tu kaunteya*
> *śītoṣṇa-sukha-duḥkha-dāḥ*
> *āgamāpāyino 'nityās*
> *tāṁs titikṣasva bhārata*

The non-permanent appearance of happiness and distress, and the other dualities and their disappearance in due course are like the appearance and disappearance of the summer and winter seasons. One must learn to tolerate them without being disturbed. Tolerance is essentially the readiness to live with unpalatable situations or unpleasant people. It is a strength that enables us to shift focus from less important things to more important things. It goes back to the point on leading our lives with a higher purpose.

- **Forgiveness:** This means being able to overlook others' faults and offences committed towards us. It is a quality that is crucial for peace and harmony in this world.

We live in the age of kali yuga, an age especially characterized by rampant inclination for quarrel and hypocrisy. If we cannot forgive others, then there is no possibility of relationships surviving on any level, whether it is between siblings, husband and wife, and friends at a micro level. At a macro level, it's between religions, various academic groups, castes and even between nations. According to great saints of all traditions, the definition of love is the capacity to forgive endlessly. The love of a parent is such that they forgive their child no matter what the child has done. If we cannot forgive, we cannot love.

- **Selfless Service:** This is a very important ingredient for us to show compassion. To be willing to selflessly serve to elevate others is an expression of love and is a manifestation of how we give without expecting anything in return. It's unconditional, as pure as a mother's love for her child. She is selfless in the way she deals with her child. That's a reflection of her compassion.

SIX

The Circus Tamer

Human Quality: Mind Control

An adventurous man climbed up a mountain to experience the sheer kick of scaling yet another peak in life. In his teens, he revelled in outdoor games and was a champion in sports in school. In his youth, that passion transformed into a flair for adventure sports like skiing, zip lining, rock climbing, day hiking, etc. He assiduously focused on physical fitness and strived to go on one arduous trek in a fortnight. He found that physically challenging himself was a means to express himself.

At the end of one such trek, he scaled one of the Shivalik ranges in Uttarakhand in northern India. As he scaled the peak, he spotted a sage meditating at a distance. Initially, he was surprised to find another person on the lone mountain peak. Although panting due to the climb, the man was curious to know how the sage got here and to know more about him. The man walked towards the sage.

As the sage opened his eyes, the man asked him, 'Sir, what are you doing at the top of this mountain in solitude?'

In deep thought, the hermit replied, 'I have a lot of work to complete here before I return to the plains.'

Puzzled, the mountaineer exclaimed, 'Work? I don't see anyone or anything around. What work are you doing here? You're just sitting here in a yoga pose.'

Calmness personified, the sage responded, 'I have to tame some wild animals—two hawks, two bears, two rabbits, one donkey and a snake.'

Clueless, the man looked around and said, 'But I don't see any animals around. Where are these wild creatures you are talking about?'

The thoughtful sage explained, 'Well, I have these two cunning hawks who always look for a prey and are eager to land on nasty places. I want to train and tame them such that they only go to good places. These two hawks are my two fault-finding eyes. I also have to subdue two mighty bears. They are always trying to snatch and attack. I need to train them not to just take but also give. These two bears are my hands.'

The man looked at the sage in awe after what he had just heard.

The hermit continued, 'I need to pacify two restless rabbits. These rabbits are always trying to avoid challenges and go only to places of comfort. These rabbits are my two legs. Then, I have to control this stubborn donkey. It refuses to work and is a very lazy fellow. It likes to rest but brays with excuses when the time to contribute arrives. This donkey is my body. But of all these beasts, the most vicious is the snake. It's no ordinary serpent for it spits venom and bites without warning, although caged. And this snake is my tongue. This toxic tongue spits out envy, anger, harsh speech, criticism and lies. And therefore, I wish to quell this deadly snake so that the venom of these spiteful tendencies can be neutralized.'

The thoughtful sage thus explained to the courageous mountaineer that the real adventure in life begins when we conquer the inner world. This struck the mountaineer with wonder.

How often have we read and discussed the importance of physical fitness? Yes, it's indeed important but we don't attribute as much importance to mental fitness and mind control.

As the Bhagavad Gita explains (2.61),

> *tāni sarvāṇi saṁyamya*
> *yukta āsīta mat-paraḥ*
> *vaśe hi yasyendriyāṇi*
> *tasya prajñā pratiṣṭhitā*

By intelligently reflecting on our experiences, we can come to the realization that our senses often push us to engage in regrettable acts. Indiscriminate sensual desires can trap us in addictions and self-defeating thought patterns. Thus, the Bhagavad Gita recommends utilizing our intelligence at every step to manage and control our mind.

Here comes the fundamental question: where do we start this journey to cultivate steady intelligence? How do we accomplish this self-mastery? To begin with, we could do that by keeping our wild animal-like senses under control and by thoughtfully engaging them positively. Great success demands great focus, which is only possible for the self-controlled.

Our self-mastery is reflected in three ways:

- **Perseverance in the midst of Adversity:** Whenever we pursue something in life, quite often we encounter reversals and adversity. That's the nature of the world and it is nevertheless difficult for us to remain unaffected by the turn of events. This is but natural. When faced with such unexpected reversals in life, Krishna advises us to learn to tolerate, as mentioned in Bhagavad Gita (2.14).

mātrā-sparśās tu kaunteya
śītoṣṇa-sukha-duḥkha-dāḥ
āgamāpāyino 'nityās
tāṁs titikṣasva bhārata

O son of Kuntī, the non-permanent appearance of happiness and distress and their disappearance in due course are like the appearance and disappearance of winter and summer seasons. They arise from sense perception, O scion of Bharata, and one must learn to tolerate them without being disturbed.

It is not easy, but this tolerance is a very important quality that a person needs to cultivate in order to sustain in the quest to accomplish what the person wants to. Tolerance enables us not to stop/to step back. Now, for us to steer forward, what sustains us is our natural love for what we do. That natural love is developed when we are able to develop a higher purpose for our own pursuits. That striving in the higher purpose is cemented by strong belief in the cause. When that foundation is well-laid, it sets in motion a powerful momentum to tide over obstacles and difficulties that ensue in our path.

- **Attention to Detail is a Symptom of Love:** When we express our genuine love for somebody, it manifests in the utmost care that we take in the experience.

Imagine inviting a dear friend home for dinner. It's not just dinner that we serve but we try to make that person feel special that evening. There is a laundry list of things that we do for the big evening: to start with, planning the dinner menu with items of the friend's choice. Sometimes, people contact a mutual friend to understand finer aspects of the friend's liking, the nitty-gritty of it all so as to make it more special. Once the menu is finalized, we put in the effort to shop for the necessary grocery items. We choose the best-in-class vegetables, fruits, cereals and dairy products to ensure that the final output is delicious. Then, we get into a mode of meditation to cook the dishes in the best possible way, with just the right amounts of spices, sugar and condiments added as ingredients. That's just the cooking. We then go the extra mile to deck out the house attractively, at least the drawing room where we spend most parts of the evening. This involves dusting, cleaning, using pleasing fragrances, etc. There could be gifts or memorabilia that we consider giving the friend. In reality, there is a lot more than what is described here. The idea conveyed here is that we get into the details of things when the feeling of love in involved. Our spontaneous enthusiasm for what we do will make us observe, analyse, improve and execute details to make our contribution world-class.

- **High Energy in Doing Desirable Things:** When we stay invested in what we do and put our heart and soul into it, the body derives energy through it. The enjoyment of absorption in what we do inundates us with high energy, which leads to our involvement in the activity thoroughly. Not just that, the enthusiasm we exhibit is contagious and arouses the interest of others as well. Coming back to the central theme of mind control, to begin with, it's important that we believe in the importance of mind control and then commit ourselves to the process. Once we are convinced and stay committed to it, our body will rigorously pursue it.

Cultivating higher intelligence through spiritual wisdom helps turn a savage into a sage of steady intelligence. Under the operational control of clear and steady intelligence, the senses happily and easily come under control to work for us and not against us.

SEVEN

The Flowing River

Human Quality: Commitment

Roshan, a young accountant, approached Keshav Acharya, a former financial planner and now a Krishna monk for two decades. Despite a successful career, Roshan felt a lack of inner fulfilment and conveyed that he was interested in exploring spirituality but was unable to devote time for spiritual practices.

'You are always so happy, composed and clear-headed,' Roshan said to Keshav, 'I wish I were a monk too. How can I cultivate spiritual consciousness like you and when will it be a good time for me to begin?'

In a matter-of-fact way, Keshav said, 'I can teach you but you will have to begin immediately.' Perplexed by the guru's response, Roshan felt the need to explain his predicament. 'It is not possible. You don't seem to know what it takes to live the life of a family man. I'm busy with so many responsibilities. I am asking for the future when I retire.'

Keshav listened patiently as Roshan explained his state of mind contemplatively. In a few minutes, they made their way to the community hall for dinner and the conversation soon changed to other topics of life. Rohan felt comforted that he didn't have to explain his predicament to the monk further.

The next day, Roshan came over to the ashram again and saw Keshav sitting on the banks of the river, gazing intently at the waters.

Roshan broached the conversation, 'Swamiji, have you dropped something here?'

Without looking away from the flowing waters, Keshav said, 'I'm waiting to cross the river.'

'So, are you waiting for a boat?' asked Roshan.

'No, each of us has to swim across the river alone,' responded Keshav.

'So, what is stopping you from swimming across the river,' Roshan smiled. 'You can swim, can't you?'

'Yes, I can,' the monk asserted, 'but I'll swim across as soon as the river's flow stops.'

Roshan poked Keshav mockingly, 'In that case, you will have to wait forever.'

The monk smiled at Roshan.

Gaining confidence, Roshan added, 'Because if it stops flowing, it isn't a river. If you are serious about crossing over, you'll have to jump into the river, swim against the flow and get on the other side. Start now; waiting won't help.'

With a reassuring smile, Keshav looked at Roshan and asserted, 'This is exactly the lesson I wanted to teach you. Spirituality does not complement life; it completes it. Our responsibilities are like the flow of a river, they will never stop. Committing to a spiritual life is a matter of committing our mind and our consciousness to a higher purpose. It does not require any extra resources or time. It's an internal adjustment.

As we cultivate spiritual knowledge, that knowledge broadens our worldview and awards us clarity. Thus, our approach to life and the effectiveness of our efforts become wholesome and progressively fruitful.'

Roshan nodded at Keshav and smiled quietly. Keshav put his hand over Rohan's shoulders and comforted him. Roshan broke out of his mental shackles and acknowledged the logic and relevance in Keshav's analogy. Roshan sought to know more on this topic. They both walked along the river bank, with Keshav elaborating more on what he meant and how Roshan could prepare himself for the mental adjustment.

Roshan's dilemma is a situation many of us encounter in life. We tend to see the spiritual and the material as two separate facets of life that need to be dealt with independently. Some, in fact, put them in separate boxes so as to pursue them at different stages of their life. In fact, it is a common thought process among a section of people that they will focus on the material aspects of life until the age of sixty–sixty-five and consider spiritual pursuits post-retirement. However, the spiritual and the material are not to be seen as separate but as one coexisting with the other. The spirit soul (ātma) is placed in a material body and it is the spiritual energy and consciousness that make the body appear lively.

Lord Krishna describes in the Bhagavad Gita (2.22),

> *vāsāṁsi jīrṇāni yathā vihāya*
> *navāni gṛhṇāti naro 'parāṇi*
> *tathā śarīrāṇi vihāya jīrṇāny*
> *anyāni saṁyāti navāni dehī*

As a person puts on new garments, giving up old ones, similarly, the soul accepts new material bodies, giving up the old and useless ones.

We have witnessed the same in own lives as we accept the continuous changes of the body from childhood to teens and from teens to youth and again from youth to old age. So, it's important that we lead our lives in such a way that we nourish both the soul (spiritually) and the body (materially).

Further, there is another verse in the *Srimad Bhagavatam* (2.4.2),

> *ātma-jāyā-sutāgāra-*
> *paśu-draviṇa-bandhuṣu*
> *rājye cāvikale nityaṁ*
> *virūḍhāṁ mamatāṁ jahau*

This verse explains that worldly life keeps us busy with eight things—our body, life partner, children, vehicles, home, money, relatives and career. Yet, unless we learn to connect with our supreme spiritual source and the true spiritual nature, we will not find real happiness despite fulfilling our physical, economical, emotional, intellectual, social and even religious longings.

Steady commitment is possible when we are willing to remain focused beyond constant changes which are unstoppable, unpredictable and uncontrollable.

The most important factor that facilitates regulation in our activities—in the way we balance material and spiritual life—is our choice of association. The dynamics of association are similar to how a sponge absorbs liquids of different colours and then releases them when squeezed.

One has to be careful in the choice of:

- **Social Media Friends:** In today's age of social media, where people network freely with strangers across the globe on multiple platforms and forge relationships, both remote and then in person, it's important to understand the deeper drivers of behaviour in people and then connect with them. Beyond social media, this can also include people in our neighbourhood, the society we live in and the people we socialize with during yoga or gym sessions, to name a few. Otherwise, a superficial approach here can create havoc. Being able to find alignment with one's purpose in life is fundamental. One should not view such friendships as casual but genuinely invest and care for the relationship. For us to be able to do it, we need to understand the person deeper.
- **Business or Professional Associates:** If one were to visit the company's page on Glassdoor, a website where current and past workers post anonymous reviews of their companies, to understand workplace experiences and reviews posted by employees, both anonymous and otherwise, one will find work-life balance as a key component in the pros section. It has been scientifically proven that work-life balance is a key determinant of mental wellness. In today's competitive work environment, where a professional spends ten hours at work on an average, it's important to choose the right associates there as well. Some people tend to spend more time at the workplace to escape domestic pressures. Some see colleagues as people beyond just business relationships—as comrades in front of whom they can

vent their feelings about work/home. In such dynamic and fading boundaries in relationships, the importance of choice becomes more pronounced.

- **Husband and Wife:** This is straightforward as this is a lifelong commitment. Building on the point made earlier, colleagues may change as we change our workplace but not the husband or wife. The highest level of care should be exercised in choosing a life partner, one who not just supports but inspires us to pursue our personal and professional goals and helps us find meaning in life in line with our defined purpose. In fact, such inspiring partners can help us reshape our purpose and help us taste success and happiness in life.

To summarize, the reason why we need to put our mind to choosing carefully when it comes to the three relationships mentioned earlier is because they have the power to influence our:

- **Values:** Values are the bedrock of what defines our behaviour and are integral to the culture we promote. When we have a robust value system, we are able to discriminate between right and wrong, and act appropriately.
- **Thoughts:** Thoughts mushroom in the mind based on how our values are defined. This is a result of the trickle-down effect, as values shape our thoughts in terms of how we respond to situations in life
- **Dealings:** Our thoughts shape our behaviour in terms of how we deal with people and build relationships. Positive

dealings build relationships, while negative dealings spoil relationships.

- **Ambitions:** As values, thoughts and dealings mount and as we lead a life, we begin to look at the world and ourselves in a certain way. Further, our expectations from life and from ourselves change course accordingly. In our quest for improvement, our ambitions are set in line with what we expect from ourselves.

Therefore, regulation of association is the mother of all regulations.

EIGHT

Leadership Means Care

Human Quality: Compassion

In the Ramayana, there is a beautiful story of how Lord Rama was once organizing food for the monkey army at a makeshift camp in the forest. Lord Rama personally organized fresh fruits, roots, drinking water and leaf plates.

Once everything was arranged, everyone was made to sit in rows as the serving team got ready to serve the meal. Practically everyone was seated, including Lord Rama. Hanumanji, however, was left standing as he found all the sitting spots occupied. Although very hungry, Hanumanji decided to wait for everyone to finish their meal and then eat alone at the end.

When Lord Rama saw this, he requested Hanumanji, 'Please come and share this plate with me.'

Flabbergasted at even the thought of the proposal, Hanumanji implored the Lord, 'My dear Lord! You are my Master. How can I share your plate?'

Lord Rama said, 'O Hanuman, it will be my greatest pleasure if you share this banana leaf with me.'

Hanumanji petitioned further, 'My Lord, I am all but a monkey, and you are the Supreme Lord, the King of Ayodhya. You treat me with affection, but I cannot treat you as if we are at the same level.'

At that moment, Lord Rama drew a line along the middle of the long banana leaf with his finger. He instructed Hanumanji, 'I am sitting here and will eat from this side of the plate. Now you sit facing me and eat from the other side of the banana leaf.' In this, way both the master and the disciple experienced the joy of eating together.

We play different roles in life, those of a spouse, child, parent, friend, etc. Besides, we are all leaders in our own capacities as a friend, an elder sibling, parent, employee, manager, business owner and so on. Leadership grants us power over our subordinates for direction and development. If we allow our ego to rule us, it can very quickly misuse a position of power by dominating or exploiting others for personal gain.

True leadership warrants that we take care of those who are under our care or dependent on us. Lord Rama took that responsibility upon himself and decided that he will share his resources with Hanumanji. Lord Rama was neither indifferent to the situation nor okay with just acknowledging it. In the absence of other resources, he was willing to share what he personally had. This is the sign of a true leader.

Compassion is the foundation of leadership.

A compassionate leader:

- **Is Exemplary:** When leaders lead by example, combined with a positive outlook, they become desirable and inspiring. Leading by example is considered a hallmark characteristic of good leadership as it conveys a strong message through action and not through words. From a team's point of view, they see the leader as a person of action, not just words and as someone who shows the way. From a leader's point of view, it helps him/her truly understand what it takes to accomplish something. When leaders get their hands dirty, they become empathetic leaders. As the term suggests, empathy leads to compassion.

- **Has Trustworthy Relationships:** Compassionate leaders embody a tangible expression of love for the feelings of others. They truly recognize what others go through in life and, as a result, genuinely take action to help others. When there is such an expression of genuine care and concern for people, leaders naturally forge relationships that are trustworthy and long-lasting.

- **Respects Others Genuinely:** There is genuineness writ large in the actions of leaders who are compassionate. At the core of their heart, they care for the people around them and respect people for who they are. They mean no harm and there is no manipulation or duplicity in their behaviour. In case they do not appreciate a certain thing or want to suggest that something should be done differently, they communicate politely and explain their reasons too.

- **Facilitates Others' Actions and Growth:** Such leaders understand that their success is a function of their team's success. Empowering their team and equipping them with resources and capabilities is a way of life for them. Because such leaders thrive in the success of others, they derive a lot of satisfaction from it. They typically invest a lot of time conversing with their team members individually and understanding what drives them, what challenges they face and how they as leaders can better intervene and enable their team members' growth, both professionally and personally.

- **Listens and Deeply Understands:** Communication is a two-way channel and these leaders understand that well. Because they are compassionate, they are keen to hear from people how they feel and what they are actually looking at. The leaders then mould their offering of care in line with what their team members are seeking. Empathy in such leaders truly comes to the fore as they listen intently and strive to deeply understand the other person's point of view.

In this story, Lord Rama demonstrated his compassion and respectful treatment of Hanumanji. It was indeed a touching gesture for Hanumanji, as he felt wonderful sharing the banana leaf with his master. So, the next time you see a banana leaf, remember the care and love shown by a true leader towards his dependant, the care shown by Lord Rama for Hanumanji. To summarize, it's important to remember that care is the ultimate foundation for leadership, according to *Srimad Bhagavatam* (9.4.65),

> *ye dārāgāra-putrāpta-*
> *prāṇān vittam imaṁ param*
> *hitvā māṁ śaraṇaṁ yātāḥ*
> *kathaṁ tāṁs tyaktum utsahe*

The Supreme Lord Himself says: 'Since pure devotees give up their homes, wives, children, relatives, riches and even their lives simply to serve Me, without any desire for material improvement in this life or in the next, how can I give up such devotees at any time?'

That's Him, demonstrating the importance of care. Let's follow in His footsteps.

NINE

The Power of Time

Human Quality: Gratitude

The Clarke family in England was like many other middle-class families in the early twentieth century. They shared similar dreams and aspirations and their most cherished desire was to go on a holiday to the US.

Their daughter had been talking about it with her friends and their son was constantly daydreaming about it. For several years, the Clarke family had been saving for their dream trip—sailing across the Atlantic to America. Finally, Mr Clarke surprised everyone one fine day at dinner with tickets for the journey in a few months' time. Excited by the imminent manifestation of their dreams, Mrs Clarke baked a cake to celebrate the occasion. The kids ran around the house, jumping on sofas in uncontainable delight.

The next day, on his way back from school, their son was thrilled over the prospect of being able to hold the ticket in his hands again. He recalled how the previous night his sister had slept with her ticket under her pillow. So, he decided to take a shortcut to reach home. He was in constant thought of the happenings at home that morning. While taking the shortcut, he fondly recalled how his sister had shared with him her dream, where she saw herself at the top of a deck looking at whales and dolphins in the ocean.

Cock-a-hoop, the boy ran into trouble while jumping over a fence. A stray dog chased him and bit his leg, leaving the boy crying in pain. Thankfully, a passerby rescued him with the help of a stick. The crying boy was quickly taken to a doctor nearby. His parents were informed by phone. Mrs Clarke was the first to reach the doctor's clinic along with her daughter. Mr Clarke reached shortly thereafter. The doctor treated the boy's wound and gave him an injection to protect him against infections. The boy was feeling better and was taken home.

A few weeks later, Mr Clarke came home from work later than normal. He looked visibly depressed and his eyes were downcast. His wife enquired if everything was all right at work. Mr Clarke explained how he had called their booking agent during the day to book a special show on the ship to celebrate her thirty-fifth birthday, which incidentally fell during the journey. During the conversation, Mr Clarke happened to mention their son's run-in with the dog. The agent changed the conversation abruptly, wanting to know more about the accident. After hearing that the boy was bitten by a stray dog and was given injections, the agent informed Mr Clarke that he would have to cancel their tickets immediately as the travel policy did not allow anyone bitten recently by an animal to travel on the ship as it posed a danger to other passengers. The agent informed him that even if the Clarkes were to reach the US, they would be placed in quarantine.

A heartbroken Mrs Clarke burst into tears but then composed herself to inform the kids upstairs. First, she spoke to her daughter since it was important she understood that her bedridden brother was not made to feel guilty. Then, Mrs Clarke approached her son, who was still receiving weekly injections for the dog bite. She made up a story about how their trip had to be cancelled that year due to some issue with the agent—that he had overbooked and was unaware of the restrictions and formalities. The boy broke down as soon as he heard the news. He had told all his friends about the forthcoming trip and was looking forward to it with bated breath. In fact, he had told his near and dear ones that he did not want anything for Christmas other than this trip.

The kids held on to their cancelled tickets and looked at them like a lost treasure. The parents stuck to the story that these tickets would be transferred to next year and that they had in fact been promised a free upgrade to compensate for the agent's mistake. Time went by.

On the day of their originally scheduled departure, the kids insisted on seeing the ship. The parents accompanied them to the harbour, to lift their spirits. The kids appeared sad but the parents tried their best to wear a smile to keep the kids' dream alive by talking about the same trip that awaited them the following year. But for now, with their dream shattered, the kids kept quiet and looked dejected as they waved goodbye to the ship as it sailed away.

A few days later, Mr Clarke rushed back home panting. He kept pressing the doorbell till Mrs Clarke opened the door. Mr Clarke yelled for the kids to come down to the drawing room immediately. Nervous, Mrs Clarke kept enquiring what the matter was. Mr Clarke continued to breathe heavily as his body shook due to what looked like a strange sense of fear. As the kids came down the stairs, Mr Clarke rushed to them. As he hugged them, he broke down in tears. Mrs Clarke had never seen her husband behave like this before. As she tried to understand what the matter was, she saw him holding a newspaper in his hands.

'The Titanic Has Sunk!' was the headline in the newspaper that Mr Clarke had been holding in his hand. Mrs Clarke's eyes turned moist as she saw her husband cry and kiss their kids.

'We were meant to be on board, honey,' cried Mr Clarke to a visibly shaken Mrs Clarke. 'We would not be together today if we had been on that ship!'

The atmosphere in the house turned to one of relief and gratitude. What a gripping story and how grateful the family felt for a certain event not happening despite craving for it and regretting missing out on it.

The *Srimad Bhagavatam* (1.9.14) describes,

> *sarvaṁ kāla-kṛtaṁ manye*
> *bhavatāṁ ca yad-apriyam*
> *sapālo yad-vaśe loko*
> *vāyor iva ghanāvaliḥ*

This verse explains how it is practically impossible to understand the movements of time. Time is all-powerful and has everyone under its grip. Just as gigantic clouds are simply swept away by a gust of wind, time sweeps away or brings forward the effects of our own karma. The time factor is so powerful and imperceptible that even the greatest and the most powerful of kingdoms and the most powerful of people can be completely crushed by one simple movement of time. Similarly, what appears to be a senseless hammering by time turns out to be a blessing in disguise later.

Time is nothing but a manifestation of the will of the Lord. It is the invisible hand of Providence delivering our karmic parcels to us, where and when it's right. Therefore, let us understand that it is extremely important for us to use each precious moment carefully, making the right and conscious decisions so that our future remains bright. Despite our best efforts and intentions, if something doesn't manifest the way we expected it to, there is no need to brood over it, as demonstrated in the story we read earlier. It's good to think that something favourable awaits us, as per the will of God. Likewise, even if something manifests as per our expectations or exceeds our expectation, we should not be proud as our efforts have been one part of a number of factors contributing to the event. Time, as the manifested will of God, has favoured us and has kindly fulfilled our desires. This should be an opportunity for us to show gratitude to God and thank Him. Such events should heighten our love for the Supreme Lord and should inspire us to find more opportunities to love Him and serve Him.

Prayer is to be considered a very important activity to include in our routine. Just as we need parents, family members and friends to express ourselves and vent our feelings, God as our Supreme Father is the one that we should constantly communicate with. Yes, prayer is an act of communicating with God. Be it the supposed good or bad times, it is a conversation between us and God, where we can talk to Him, glorify Him, thank Him, seek help from Him and request Him for strength.

The effects of deep prayer are:

- **Soothing:** Mediation on the ultimate certainty (God) in all of existence elevates us above the anxiety-ridden uncertainties of life and soothes our heart. Often times, because we genuinely vent our feelings on God, we feel that a load is off our hearts and that indeed soothes us at a subconscious level.

- **Satisfying:** Meditation on sense objects is dissatisfying and prayers connect us to the reservoir of pleasure, giving us deep satisfaction. By sense objects, we refer to things in this material world that we so often interact with and engage in. However, if we connect with God, (Rama, meaning reservoir of pleasure), who is the source of pleasure, it satisfies the heart and we feel a sense of renewed energy within us.

- **Strengthening:** Prayer replenishes our inner energy stock and strengthens us. That we connect with the Supreme Person infuses in us the strength to tackle the different challenges we encounter in life. At a subconscious level, the mind acknowledges that God is receptive to our problems and it steadies the mind against any panic troubling us from within.

- **Sublimating:** Prayerful meditation cleanses and sublimates our mind above the impurity and immorality of materialistic culture. In today's world, where we are exposed to a lot of negativity, prayer acts as a cleanser and, over time, helps us transcend the material strata in terms of how we get influenced and swayed by it. Hence, prayer should be seen as our consistent investment of time in the Divine.

TEN

Wisdom Is More Important than Logic

Human Quality: Mindfulness

Santosh, a young man, approached a guru and said, 'Please accept me as your disciple.'

The guru asked, 'What is your qualification?'

The young man said, 'I am very intelligent!'

The guru thought gravely and stated a case study for Santosh to examine. The guru presented the case study to Santosh, 'Two men come out of a chimney. The face of one man was blackened, while the other man's face was clean. Which man would wash his face first?'

Santosh said confidently, 'Well, the one with the blackened face.'

The guru disagreed and explained, 'When they came out of the chimney, both men looked at each other. The man with the blackened face thought, "This man has a clean face, so my face should also be clean." But the man with the clean face thought, "Oh, his face has gone black. My face must also be black." Thus, he will clean his face first.'

Hearing this, Santosh requested the guru, 'Please give me one more chance.'

The guru agreed and gave him another chance to prove himself, 'Two men go down a chimney. One comes out with a blackened face and the other with a clean face. Who would wash his face first?'

Santosh replied immediately, 'The one with the clean face.'

The guru responded, 'No, the one with the blackened face.' He elaborated, 'When they came out, both looked at each other. The man with the blackened face thought to himself, "This man has a clean face even after climbing down a chimney. Maybe, I am not as lucky as him. So, I should clean my face immediately before someone makes fun of me." And thus, he would promptly wash his face.'

The prospective disciple, now charged with a new sense of logic, said, 'Please give me one more chance.'

The guru agreed again and stated the same scenario, 'Two men come out of a chimney. One had a blackened face and the other a clean face. Who would wash his face first?'

Confused, Santosh said, 'The one with the blackened face.'

The guru calmly replied, 'No, both will clean their face together.' He explained, 'When the man with the blackened face goes to wash his face, the man with the clean face will join him. So, both clean their faces together.'

Still wanting to prove himself, the young man requested, 'Please give me one last chance.'

The guru repeated the question, 'Two men come out of a chimney. One has a blackened face and the other a clean face. Who would wash his face first?'

Santosh, with hope in his eyes, guessed, 'Both!'

The guru replied, 'No! Neither of the men would wash their face.' He explained, 'When both come out of the chimney, they observe each other. The one with the clean face thinks, "Oh, poor guy! His face has become black. I should not say anything, lest I embarrass him." And the man with the blackened face thinks, "Oh! His face is clean. Perhaps mine is too." Thus, neither of them will wash their faces.'

At this point, the guru enlightened Santosh, 'Two men can never enter a chimney at the same time because of the tight space. Before you put your abilities on display, you should have understood that my question itself was foolish. Therefore, please understand that your mind cannot solve all problems for you in life. It is, in fact, wisdom that should steer intelligence in the right direction.'

Santosh admitted to the fallacy of his thought and bowed down to seek blessings from the guru.

There is a beautiful verse from the *Chaitanya Charitamrita* (Madhya Lila 25.57), which illustrates how intellectual arguments and logical inference alone remain inconclusive in trying to find the truth:

> *tarko 'pratiṣṭhaḥ śrutayo vibhinnā*
> *nāsāv ṛṣir yasya mataṁ na bhinnam*
> *dharmasya tattvaṁ nihitaṁ guhāyāṁ*
> *mahājano yena gataḥ sa panthāḥ*

Logic and intelligence can be twisted to prove anything that one wants to and thus remain inconclusive in ascertaining the truth. It is spiritual wisdom that helps us use the tools of logic and intelligence properly and wholesomely. This spiritual wisdom can be cultivated in the association of wise persons who have realized that truth through honest and unpretentious practice. The saintly of compassionate heart, who have realized the truth, can take us to the destination of that truth. The journey to the destination of truth begins by giving one's sincere attention to the instructions of great souls and by putting those instruction into practice for personal realization of the truth.

Vidura Niti, narrated in the form of a dialogue between Vidura and King Dhritarashtra, is considered the precursor in some ways of *Chanakya Niti*. Vidura is held to be a paragon of truth, dutifulness, impartial judgement and steadfast dharma. He is considered the embodiment of the inner consciousness of the Mahabharata. Vidura Niti is Vidura's instructions on morality and Vidura is considered to be not just a personification of wisdom and an extremely wise person but also an extraordinary friend, rather a tireless friend who hopes for the well-being of Dhritarashtra even though Dhritarashtra repeatedly rebuffs the advice given to him by Vidura.

This is an excerpt from Vidura Niti:

'A wise king should discriminate the two with the help of one. He must control the three by means of four. He has to conquer the five, know the six, abstain from the seven and thus he'll be happy. By one, it means intelligence. By two, the right and the wrong. Three: friend, stranger and enemy. By four is meant: gift, conciliation, disunion and severity. By five, the senses. By six, treaty, war, etc. By seven, women, dice, hunting, harshness of speech, drinking, severity of punishment and waste of wealth.'

Further, the Vidura Niti specifies sixteen symptoms of wise action:

- **Exert the Best of One's Might:** The wise put their best foot forward and there should be no hesitation once a decision has been taken. One is directed by the right knowledge and decides the course of action accordingly.
- **Act to the Best of One's Might:** There is no room for half measures when it comes to taking action. One should make every effort and leave the rest to God in terms of how the final outcome manifests itself.
- **Disregard Nothing as Insignificant:** The wise value each and everything. There is a complacency that they exhibit but they prepare to face any challenge that can surround them.
- **Understand Quickly:** The wise are sharp and have a high grasping power. They derive this power from constant tapas and meditation that they do on the Supreme.
- **Listen Patiently:** The wise are always on a quest for knowledge as they strive for constant learning and development of their personality. As a result, they listen to people patiently and imbibe the valuable inputs received.
- **Pursue Objects with Judgement and Not from Desire:** The wise are objective in their approach to life and not swayed by sense gratification that manifest in the form of desires. While they do have desires and are ambitious, they consistently do a needs-assessment analysis for them to accomplish their ambitions. They judge the situation at all times and pursue what is feasible according to the best of their efforts.

- **Mind One's Own Business:** The wise are so focused on their pursuit and work hard that they don't have time to poke their nose into others' affairs. In fact, that's not even in the consideration set. They share advice in the form of suggestions, when solicited.

- **Do Not Strive for Objects That Are Unattainable:** As earlier discussed, the wise pursue with sound judgement and, as a result, remain realistic in their goals setting. They have the power to discriminate between what is attainable and what is not, of course, without any compromise when it comes to their efforts.

- **Do Not Grieve for What Is Gone and Lost:** The wise look ahead, always. Even in times of introspection, they reflect with an intent to learn from experience and strive to apply the learnings for the future. They do repent over sins or mistakes committed unknowingly. Repentance is considered an act in the mode of goodness (satva guna) when one genuinely begs for mercy from God, cleanses any impurities and earnestly strives to be more careful to not repeat the same mistake in the future.

- **Have Clarity of Mind in Calamity:** The wise understand that their effort is only one contributor to the final outcome of the situation. They follow the principle as elicited by Lord Krishna in the Bhagavad Gita (18.14), where He describes the five factors of action: the place of action [the body], the performer, the various senses, the many different kinds of endeavours and ultimately the Super soul. Firm belief and absorption in this principle provides them clarity of mind. So when calamity strikes, they understand the situation around them as something beyond their control and they focus only on what is in their control.

- **Complete the Task Once Begun:** The wise have no room for lethargy as they determinedly focus on the task at hand. They do the groundwork and prepare well in advance. Once they have begun, they don't give up and persist to complete the tasks by manoeuvring through different challenges that they encounter along the way.

- **Never Waste Time:** The wise understand that time is precious, as it can never be regained once lost. As a result, they value time immensely to constantly channelize their energy in the right direction, be it learning, building something, serving for the sake of a good cause and making a positive difference to the lives of people around them.

- **Honest in Their Work:** Integrity is a key attribute of the wise. They do what they say (integrity) and they say what they do (honesty). They admit to the fallacy that they observe and work towards course correction.

- **Never Sneer at What Is Good:** The wise have no sense of inferiority complex in them. Due to their broad mind, they openly appreciate the good in others and pursue to learn from them.

- **Equipoised in Success and Failure:** The wise understand that nature of material life is relative, sometimes cyclical too, and that success and failure, similar to happiness and sadness, are like the changing seasons in a year. The wise recognize that whatever happens in life is as per the will of God and they take whatever comes in their stride, with equipoise, calmness and composure. They don't get overwhelmingly excited.

- **Aware of People's Nature, Their Actions and Connections between Actions:** The wise are keen observers. They watch people and events closely. In that process, they are able to identify patterns in people's behaviour, their interactions and their actions, and are able to connect the right dots. This awareness of the exterior world formulates, in a way, their approach to work and life.

ELEVEN

Hoping against Hope

Human Quality: Positive Thinking

Amritlal, a middle-aged businessman living in the suburbs of Mumbai, was under a lot of debt. With multiple creditors chasing him every second day, he was in a state of despair and utter hopelessness. As he was walking past a park, depressed and unable to figure out what to do, an old gentleman walked up to him and said, 'Do you need some money?'

Amritlal responded, 'Yes.'

'Here, take this cheque!' the gentleman said, 'I'm offering you Rs 1 crore.'

The businessman couldn't believe what was happening to him. In utter disbelief, he looked at the cheque for Rs 1 crore signed by 'G.D. Birla'. Soon, the gentleman walked away.

Flabbergasted, Amritlal couldn't believe his eyes and looked up at the Almighty for the godsend help. He gathered the energy from within and was brimming with hope and confidence. He felt that the world around him had changed miraculously. He felt good like he'd never felt before. Just as he was about to take the cheque to the bank, he told himself, 'Should I avail the amount now? This will be a debt that I'll have to repay. So, let me keep this as backup while I work on a new business plan and apply myself.'

He returned home and kept the cheque in the safe. Invigorated, he applied himself fully to making a new business plan and remained committed to bringing his ideas to life. Whenever he found the going tough, he told himself, 'I have Rs 1 crore given by Mr Birla and that remains with me.'

With this confidence, Amritlal worked hard, strategized and put together a small team to begin with. Within three months, he observed a turnaround in his business. Over time, he expanded his team in a big way. In five months, his business brought in enough revenue and he repaid all his creditors. With this positive reversal, he felt very good. Just then, he thought about the cheque for Rs 1 crore in his safe. In fact, he heaved a sigh of relief that it wasn't a part of his debt. He was glad that he had kept it aside. He decided to return the cheque and the timely help offered by Mr Birla.

So Amritlal went to the same place where he had received the cheque. Just as he was about to enter the park, he spotted Mr Birla coming from the opposite side. Amritlal's face brightened and there was a wide smile on his face as Mr Birla approached him.

Amritlal walked a few paces, waved the cheque in front of Mr Birla and said, 'Sir, I can't thank you enough for your timely help but I didn't have to use it as I was able to turn things around myself. Still, thank you and please take this cheque back.'

Just as the businessman was about to hand over the cheque, a nurse came over. The nurse touched Mr Birla on the shoulder and pulled him back saying, 'Please return to your place, sir.'

Amritlal requested the nurse, 'Let me hand over the cheque to him. Then, he can leave.'

She looked at Amritlal and said, 'Please don't tell me he issued you a cheque signed in the name of G.D. Birla.'

Sensing that something was amiss, Amritlal replied, 'Yes, he did. Here it is.'

The nurse said, 'Sorry sir. I'm a nurse. He has intellectual disability. For years, he has had this habit of meeting strangers and issuing them cheques in the name of G.D. Birla.'

'Oh, I see,' Amritlal sighed.

'Sorry, sir. We let him do it as it keeps him calm and happy.'

A bewildered Amritlal smiled at her, patted the old man on his back and started to walk back slowly. He was in deep thought. He was trying to fathom what had happened in his life over the past five months. He was puzzled and amused by the source of his hope, who had instilled in him the confidence and power he needed to put his plans into action.

After deep thought, Amritlal told himself, 'It's all in the mind and how we put our senses into action.'

This story is a classic example of the power of positive thinking. Logically speaking, the situation around him didn't change one bit but the conditioning of his mind transformed due to his perceived understanding of the situation in a certain way. This, in a way, also reflects the power of positive thoughts. So much so that in this case he catapulted his business to successful heights like never before. Positive thoughts are the springboard that we should leverage in difficult times.

My spiritual master, H.H. Radhanath Swami, describes the four principles of positive thinking as follows:

- **Acceptance:** Accepting an unfortunate situation as a reality beyond our control is the beginning of the journey of positivity. When certain situations take a turn for the worse, we may artificially psyche ourselves up with false assurances that things are just as fine as before. This is an immature response to the inevitable downturns of this world. When things or people change, denial makes the pain acute. We may offer a cosmetic smile, remain gung-ho and give a pep talk to ourselves but the seething pain will corrode us from within. Accepting an unfortunate turn of events as the inevitable outcome beyond our control takes the steam off a potentially stressful situation. However simple it may sound, it is the most challenging of the four steps.

  The strength to accept the bitter truths of life comes if we are anchored to the absolute truth, the Truth of God, and our sweet and loving relationship with Him. A culture of prayers and chanting of God's names gives us the strength to accept disturbing events and remain peaceful and sober even during emotionally painful periods of our lives.

- **Optimism:** However bad the situation is, there's always a silver lining. We need to look for a possible good outcome of an apparently tragic or negative event. American philanthropist W. Clement Stone said, 'There is little difference in people, but that little difference makes a big difference. The little difference is attitude. The big difference is whether it's positive or negative.' If we hope for a better future, even in the middle of a hopeless mess, we are placing our tender hearts in the hands of our benevolent God. He will then work wonders in our lives. We should look for that silver lining in the cloud even when the situation appears negative.

- **Gratitude:** Our life is a constant flow of blessings. If we can simply thank God and other people for all the gifts that we are constantly receiving, we'll remain positive rather than being cynical. Cynicism drains our vital energy, whereas gratitude keeps our life simple, heart purer and mind peaceful. As life treats us badly, we should focus on things that life has given us, although we may be undeserving of them. 'I had no shoes and I complained until I met a man with no feet' is a famous quote and a sacred tool of a grateful mind. Gratitude certainly helps us rise above cynical tendencies.

- **Appreciation:** Genuine appreciation and encouragement spreads positivity and joy. Kind words of encouragement and sincere appreciation of others emit positive energy everywhere, especially to those who come in close contact with us. Appreciation creates a virtuous cycle of positivity. As we make others happy, positive and charged up, they in turn inject in others the contagious quality of spreading positivity. Overall, this builds a positive environment where one can lead a meaningful life centred on spiritual principles and integrity. The world is filled with people who check on others when they make a mistake but a spiritual leader focuses on the right things that others do. The leader then fans the spark of goodness.

Let me share an example. A few years ago, many people spoke at an ISKCON programme in Mumbai that was attended by thousands of devotees. The speakers were friends and students of H.H. Radhanath Swami. They appreciated him profusely for impacting their lives in a positive way with his personal touch. Later, when it was H.H. Radhanath Swami's turn to speak, he surprised everybody by speaking about each and every member there, recalling the minute details of their wonderful qualities. He vividly recalled incidents and exchanges that had taken place over twenty-five years ago. So much so that he even mentioned those who had cooked dosas and idlis for him! While driving back, when we expressed amazement at his incredible memory, his answer humbled and inspired us.

He said, 'These special souls have done so much service over the years. And if I don't remember their love, sacrifice, and affection, my life is condemned.' It is adherence to these simple but sacred principles that help us connect with ourselves and others.

That evening, I learnt this very important lesson from my guru on the importance of gratitude.

TWELVE

Moments—Make Them Count!

Human Quality: Relationships

A young couple, married for three years, had been enjoying their married life so much so that they couldn't live without each other even for a day. Suddenly, things turned bitter. They began fighting over little things. However, internally, they didn't like the way things had changed between them.

It was their fourth wedding anniversary. The husband, Raj, left for work early in the morning. He was unable to meet his wife, Anisha, before leaving for work. That evening, Anisha waited for Raj to show up. She kept wondering whether he remembered that it was their anniversary that day. Just then, the doorbell rang. With bated breath, in anticipation of Raj's arrival, she ran towards the door. Just as she reached the door, she paused to catch her breath to avoid showing her excitement in front of Raj.

It was raining outside that day. Fulfilling her expectations, a soaked but smiling Raj stood at the door with a bunch of flowers in his hands. Her joy knew no bounds. She was thrilled and hugged him. The mood changed to one of joy. Both were happy and turned nostalgic, reliving their days of yore. They decided to follow it up with dinner accompanied by light music. As she was getting the table ready for dinner, the telephone in the bedroom rang. Anisha went to attend the call.

A man on the other side said, 'Hello, ma'am. I am calling from the police station. Is this Mr Raj's residence?'

She replied in the affirmative.

He responded, 'I am sorry ma'am, but there was an accident and we have an unidentified body.'

Anisha couldn't believe her ears. She peeped into the dining room right away.

The policeman continued, 'We got this number from his wallet. Please can you come to the police station to identify the body.'

Her heart sank. She was shocked. She said in a shaky voice, 'But my husband is with me at home.'

The policeman replied, 'Sorry ma'am but this accident took place at 3 p.m. while he was attempting to board the metro.'

Anisha was about to lose consciousness. She thought to herself, 'How could this happen?' She then recalled reading about how the soul of a person comes to meet a loved one before leaving the body. Dropping the phone, she rushed to the dining room to look for Raj. He wasn't there. Next, she went into the drawing room. Then, she rushed to the main door, just in case he had stepped out. He wasn't there either.

Her heart was pounding. He her confidence was shaken. She thought, 'Oh my God! It is true. He has left me for good. It was his soul that came to bid me goodbye.'

She was sweating profusely and she felt as if this was the end of the world for her and that every aspect of her life was doomed. She fell down at the main door and hit her forehead in disgust: 'Oh God! I will gladly die for another chance to make up for every little fight we have had and apologize to him.'

In deep pain, she cried profusely, 'I have lost my chance! Forever!'

A few seconds later, the bathroom door opened. Raj came out and said, 'Darling, let's have dinner.'

Seeing her pale face, he questioned her in a mellow voice, 'What happened to you?'

Anisha couldn't believe her eyes. She touched him. His hand, his body and then his face.

'What happened? Why are you crying?' he asked her, curious.

'No . . . But . . . the police called. Your wallet . . .' she stammered.

'Oh! I am sorry,' he comforted her, 'Actually, I forgot to tell you that my wallet got stolen today at the metro station.'

Relieved, she hugged him tight and apologized to him.

Life might not give everyone a second chance. So, it's important to never waste a moment when we can still make up for the wrongs we have done. Let's live life with no regrets and be honest in relationships. They say that marriages are made in heaven. As of 2018, 44 per cent of the marriages end in divorces globally. Luxemburg has the dubious distinction of a divorce rate of 87 per cent.[1] In such torrid times that we live in, it's worth scrolling

---

[1] See https://www.indiatoday.in/education-today/gk-current-affairs/story/india-has-the-lowest-divorce-rate-in-the-world-1392407-2018-11-20.

up the pages of our Vedic scriptures to look for valuable lessons in them.

In *Srimad Bhagavatam* (3.23.2), there is a verse from the story of Kardama Muni and his beloved wife, Devahūti.

> *viśrambheṇātma-śaucena*
> *gauraveṇa damena ca*
> *śuśrūṣayā sauhṛdena*
> *vācā madhurayā ca bhoḥ*

This verse describes the cordial relationship between a couple and elucidates on the seven secrets of nurturing a successful marital relationship.

These seven secrets are:

- **Intimacy (viśrambhena):** Intimacy indicates a mood of friendliness, trust and faith. A couple is to be viewed as intimate friends of each other. This intimacy manifests in the way that they deal with each other, with absolute transparency and loyalty. This also takes shape in the unalloyed service that they do for each other selflessly and always explore ways to please the other person.
- **Purity of Mind and Body (ātma-śaucena):** Purity of mind and body is accomplished by harmonizing thoughts, words and actions to become one and the same. In married life, there is no room for selfish thoughts— the 'I, me and mine' thought process. It's important that couples always seek to share what they do in life. Beyond just sharing life, if they keep Krishna (God) at the centre of all that they do and channelize all that they do in line

with an attitude to please God, that is their success in married life.

- **Great Respect (gauraveṇa):** Respect is at the core of any relationship. There is no superior or inferior position in a relationship. A couple needs to see one another as children of God and respect each other's uniqueness, individuality, backgrounds, nature, choices, strengths and development areas. With an attempt to leverage each other and combine as a team, they should invest in each other, discuss and draw from each another's strengths and help the other in their areas of development. Further, they need to be wary that familiarity can breed contempt.

- **Control the Senses (damena):**
  o **the urge to speak:** Often in relationships, partners tend to speak more than they listen. For enhanced communication and to help a relationship prosper, a robust two-way communication needs to be in place. Listening intently is a subtle way of showing care. Constantly speaking without listening is an explicit display of selfishness.

  o **the urge to get angry:** Even if there is provocation, one should remain tolerant for once one becomes angry, the whole body becomes polluted. Yes, anger is a pollutant. Anger is a product of the mode of passion and lust, so one who seeks to be transcendentally situated should check on the ability to control one's anger. As they say, anger is one letter short of danger and it can ruin relationships built over years in a matter of seconds.

- o **the urge to be attracted to any relationship outside marriage:** Fidelity in marriage is non-negotiable. Infidelity is sinful and against the ethos of marriage. Thoughts of any relationship outside of marriage are a symptom of rampant distrust in the relationship and must be quelled instantly or, as they say, nipped in the bud. Such a person should open a channel of transparent communication with the spouse right away. If matters are worse, he/she should reach out to elders in the family and settle matters amicably.

- **Service (śuśrūṣayā):** Love means doing service without selfish consideration. Love means experiencing pain to give pleasure to the person one is serving. Both the husband and wife must define their scope of service amicably and share their life with mutual care and consideration for each other's responsibilities and priorities.

- **Well Wishes (sauhṛdena):** When compassion is at the core of the relationship, one always wishes the other person well, derives pleasure in the success tasted by the spouse and explores ways to support the spouse in his or her pursuits. There should be absolutely no hidden motive.

- **Sweet Words (vācā madhurayā):** True love blooms from the heart and nourishes the exchange as one speaks sweet words as an act of expressing affection for the partner. Such an exchange impacts the partner positively, reinforces trust and nurtures the relationship further.

THIRTEEN

Do You Have This Blood Group?

Human Quality: Positive Thinking

A professor entered a class and said to all the students, 'I am going to conduct a surprise test.'

He distributed blank sheets of paper to everybody. When the students gathered their sheets of paper, they noticed that they were completely blank, barring one area in the middle—there was one black spot right in the middle of the sheet.

The professor said, 'Please write about whatever you see and observe, analyse it in your own words and express it.'

In this way, the students started writing. After the test ended, the professor collected the answer sheets. Later that evening, when the professor was reviewing the answer sheets, he observed that practically everybody had discussed in great detail only about the black dot. There were different types of responses:

'The black dot is in the centre . . .'

'The black dot is very, very tiny . . .'

'The black dot is not as intense as it looks . . .'

And so on . . .

It was nothing but their individual analysis of the black spot. Nothing more, nothing less. The professor returned to class the next day.

He looked at all the students and said, 'I gave you these sheets of paper which simply had a small, insignificant speck of a black dot,' he pointed to it, 'But, each one of you only focused on that black dot and only wrote about it.'

He paused, leaving the students to ponder over his statement.

'Why couldn't any of you see the rest of the white paper and write anything about that?'

Amazed, the students looked at each other in deep thought.

Is it not how we lead our lives sometimes? Our life has so many positive aspects, like the white sheet of paper, but we only look at the problems. Those problems, anxieties, stresses, challenges, difficulties, etc., are just like that black dot. We somehow become so obsessed with those difficulties and challenges. And as we relentlessly remain focused on those problems alone, our attention is simply fixed on those problems, difficulties, challenges, issues, shortcomings and failures, and we fail to focus and appreciate all the positive and wonderful things that have happened with us and fail to express gratitude for all the grace we have received.

There are six visions with which we see others in our interactions:

- **To See a Little Bad and Magnify It:** Such a vision extrapolates what is minutely visible and creates negativity in the mind. This leads to the person overthinking and brooding over what is not actually present.

- **To See Only Bad:** This is a blackout state of the first vision, where one zooms into the negative element completely and fails to look at anything else. Such a vision creates a situation of doom in life and one feels like someone or something has wreaked havoc in one's life.
- **To See Good and Bad but Select Bad:** This vision is certainly better than the first and second type. However, because of insecurity and lack of courage to face challenges, one focuses on the negative and that gradually erodes hope in one's mind. People with such a vision can be coached by optimists and with constant association, they can focus only on the good in others.
- **To See Good and Bad but Select Good:** People with such a vision tend to be judgemental in conversations with people and develop paranoia in their dealings with people. With paranoia writ large in their minds during conversations, they don't respond on the face value of the exchange but the 'bad' seen mars their vision and leads to avoidable misunderstandings. Left unchecked, it can lead to enmity.
- **To See Only Good:** This is a vision where one sees only the good in others and is not influenced by the apparent bad in others. While this is certainly better than the four visions mentioned earlier, the challenge here is that one is appreciative only when the apparent good is visible. Otherwise, one may possibly remain indifferent without being encouraging or exhibiting positive energy in conversations.
- **To See a Little Good and Magnify It:** This is the best vision as one focuses exclusively on even the little spark

of good seen in others and encourages them to display goodness more often. People with such a vision are immune to the so-called bad displayed by others. Rather, they inspire the other person with positivity and motivating tone of speech to get better in life. They tolerate provoking situations and continue to invest in people. Greatness lies in our ability to develop this vision at all times.

And therefore, it is said in the *Srimad Bhagavatam* (3.19.36),

tam sukhārādhyam ṛjubhir
ananya-śaraṇair nṛbhiḥ
kṛtajñaḥ ko na seveta
durārādhyam asādhubhiḥ

When we receive something positive, let us experience it and express it. If we fail to experience that positivity, we also fail to express it. Therefore, we have unlimited reasons to feel grateful and celebrate but we fail to see them. Let us try to transform our vision so that although there may be apparent challenges and difficulties and causes of negativity, we don't focus on the black spot but view that bright white sheet of paper which is full of scope for learning, opportunities for growth, occasions to celebrate and to express gratitude.

Let us remember the blood group B +. If we are not in the mood to remain positive, we will be overwhelmed by an avalanche of negativity and therefore I say that this is one of the best blood groups with respect to attitude. 'Be positive' and this positivity will save you from being overwhelmed by thoughts of negativity to truly help realize your potential.

FOURTEEN

Connecting with Right Blessings

Human Quality: Positive Thinking

A great sage and his disciples were once touring different lands in the region. The sage came across a prince, who was unabashedly indulging in sense gratification.

Observing the prince, the sage immediately told him, '*Rāja-putra ciraṁ jīva* [O prince, may you live forever].'

Then he moved ahead. His disciples follow suit. Next, they came across an ascetic who was in deep meditation and lived in extremely austere conditions. Looking at the ascetic, the sage said, '*Muni-putra mā jīva, O sage* [May you not live long, O ascetic].'

Then as the sage marched forward, he noticed a very powerful spiritual personality spreading the word of God all across the region.

The sage approached and told him, '*Jīva vā māra vā* [Whether you live or you die, it is the same thing].'

The sage then travelled further and came across a hunter. Seeing the hunter, the sage said, '*Mā jīva mā māra* [do not live, do not die].'

In this way, the sage continued his journey.

One of disciples who was observing these blessings was puzzled by the nature of the blessings the sage had showered upon each of these persons they had encountered. They were distinct but he could not correlate the blessing with the nature of the activity performed by each of the receiver of the blessing. The disciple was tempted to seek clarification. In a quiet voice, he politely asked the sage, 'Guruji, I have a doubt.'

'Sure,' the sage acknowledged. 'Please state your doubt.'

The disciple continued, 'What is the meaning behind these blessings? They were distinct and I couldn't correlate the nature of the blessing with the activity of the receiver of the blessing. Please can you elaborate?'

The sage nodded and explained, 'You see, I first came across this prince who was engaged in heavy sense gratification and so I blessed him saying "may you live forever". That's because when someone indulges in sense gratification, they die and go to hellish conditions, where they live longer. As long as one is living and enjoying one's senses, that is a period of pleasure because after that they will have to suffer the consequences of what they have done. Therefore, long life is better for him.'

The disciples around him nodded.

The sage continued, 'When I met the ascetic, I blessed him saying "may you die". That's because then he would attain eternal life and that would be the end of austerities of this life, and then he would achieve the fruits of those austerities.'

The disciples continued to listen in wonder.

The sage added, 'When I met the travelling preacher, I said that whether he lives or dies, in both situations, he is serving society by spreading positive and powerful spiritual consciousness, and therefore it doesn't matter. In both situations, he is spreading positivity around him. Therefore, I said "*Jīva vā māra vā*". Hope that's clear.'

The disciples responded in the affirmative.

'Finally, when I met the hunter, I saw that he was giving great pain to these animals. Because of the pain he was giving to the animals during his lifetime, he was becoming an instrument of pain and after this life he was going to suffer in hell and experience pain. Therefore, I said "may you neither live nor die".'

The disciples prostrated before the saint and sought his blessings. As they got up, they thanked him for enlightening them.

Many modern-day thinkers, philosophers and influencers conveniently desist from pronouncing their views on death. Even the so-called life coaches who are expected to coach leaders on life holistically stay away from the topic of death. Even if a few of them do express their thoughts, they see death as the end of life. Death need not be seen as an inconvenient truth but the ultimate meditation to reinstate clarity and perspective into every aspect of our life.

Lord Krishna expounds this tough concept in the Bhagavad Gita (2.13),

> *dehino 'smin yathā dehe*
> *kaumāraṁ yauvanaṁ jarā*
> *tathā dehāntara-prāptir*
> *dhīras tatra na muhyati*

He articulates, 'As the embodied soul continuously passes, in this body, from childhood to youth to old age, the soul similarly passes into another body at death. A sober person is not bewildered by such a change.'

Death is just another episode in one's life. Other episodes in life include formation of life in the womb of a mother, the growth of an infant into a toddler, attaining puberty, getting married, parenthood, etc. For us to understand death as just another episode, we need to first understand two words in the sentence above—'one's' and 'life'. 'One's' refers to the spiritual spark and soul that infuses life or consciousness into the body that is visible to the naked eye. The journey of the soul, referred to as life, transcends its position within a body. Unfortunately, in modern day parlance, we restrict the scope of the term 'life' to the journey of the soul within one body (the current body). At the stroke of death, the soul continues its journey into the next body, which is obtained based on the good deeds (punya) and the bad deeds (paap) performed along with desires that permeate. Together, they constitute as the state of mind that one is in.

Krishna confirms this in the Bhagavad Gita (8.6),

yaṁ yaṁ vāpi smaran bhāvaṁ
tyajaty ante kalevaram
taṁ tam evaiti kaunteya
sadā tad-bhāva-bhāvitaḥ

Whatever state of being one remembers when he quits his body, O son of Kuntī, that state he will attain without fail.

This travel in the material world is an opportunity for us to cleanse ourselves to reinstate us (the soul) back in the eternal spiritual kingdom of God, where there is no death or the transmigration of the soul. In the spiritual world, there is always eternal happiness and bliss for the soul to experience, without having to experience despair, disease, decay and death.

Now, with this complete understanding of death, we don't need to view death as an inconvenient truth but as the ultimate meditation to reinstate clarity and perspective into every aspect of life. We can approach this episode called death in multiple ways and act in more pleasing ways, exuding determination and focus. Let me elaborate:

- **Priority:** Death should remind us of the critical things that we should pursue before time strips away our possessions, positions and profiles. Our priority should be to perform only punya, remove impurities from the mind and cultivate good qualities so as to be in the right frame of mind and qualified to enter the eternal spiritual world.
- **Urgency:** Death should urge us to pursue spiritual priorities with rigour and the prospect of time killing us should prevent us from wasting time. Birth and death are two episodes that can never be timed by man. We should approach every moment in preparation for death.
- **Humility:** We have all heard the phrase 'as sure as death'. No matter what position one holds in life—be it a rich businessperson or a military chief or a popular film star or even as the president of a country—death strikes every living being without bias. The utter powerlessness to control death should make us realize our lack of

control and accept the reality with freedom and peace of mind. Death is a leveller and makes us realize the fleeting nature of the so-called gifts or riches of life. Yuktavairagya, meaning dovetailing the talents or gifts in the service of God, is the right approach to life. This will enable us to remain grounded by understanding our real position as one of the infinite children of God, who has bestowed these riches or talents or gifts upon us out of His causeless mercy.

- **Clarity:** Sometimes, we fail to appreciate people taking their positive impact on us for granted. Subconsciously lacking gratitude, we mostly tend to focus on their faults. However, the prospect of their impending absence in the form of death should make us realize that the life of the soul in a certain body is short. Not just short, but the duration is unknown as well. As a result, we should attribute a sense of value to people, express our gratitude to them and genuinely make efforts to make them feel special.

- **Immunity:** In front of the greatest fear in life, i.e., death, all other fears in life should pale into insignificance. We can thereby unshackle ourselves from the pangs of mental anxiety and fleeting situational difficulties. We should develop an attitude of 'this too shall pass' and hence uplift ourselves to focus on the highest principles of spiritual wisdom. This focus on spiritual wisdom should help us transcend from fear of death to embracing death as a pathway to developing higher consciousness as we transmigrate to newer bodies.

- **Opportunity:** Following the understanding that death is a pathway, it's to be seen as an opportunity that God has bestowed upon us to take on newer opportunities, beckoning us as we take on bodies with a higher level of consciousness. This can be understood with an analogy: after many months of winter, we feel wonderful when we get into lighter clothes at the dawn of spring. The rays of the sun and the blooming of flowers infuse positivity in us. Likewise, death is not the end but a window to opportunities beckoning us. Whether we leverage that opportunity and make it better for us or not is entirely in our hands, in our mindset and in our actions.

FIFTEEN

Endless Cycle of Desires

Human Quality: Selflessness

A happy couple dined out to celebrate their fortieth wedding anniversary. They were seen in their society as one of the best and made-for-each-other couples, complementing each other more often than not. They had two lovely children: a daughter and son, both married and settled abroad with children. Still in the pink of health and deeply in love with each other, the couple wanted to celebrate their fortieth wedding anniversary in a special way. It was a moonlight dinner along the seashore on a fine spring evening.

Just as they had placed the order for a starter and moved into a friendly conversation, a fairy suddenly emerged from the locket held by the lady. Her sudden appearance shook the couple.

The fairy smiled at the couple and said, 'You are God's gifted couple. I am truly inspired by seeing the love, loyalty, trust and devotion that you have for each other. To be able to remain together with so much affection for forty years is incredible.'

The couple smiled at each other and then at the fairy too.

The man nodded, 'Thank you. It's my good fortune to have a wife like her. She has seen me go through all the ups and downs in life. She's stood beside me all through and has been my pillar of support.' Turning emotional, he added, 'There have been times when I felt the world was against me, including God, but she lent me her support. I owe her a lot.'

The woman caressed him affectionately, 'We truly are made for each other.'

As they say, there was love in the air that had literally turned into a fairy tale of sorts.

The fairy continued, 'It's wonderful to see you together and how you complement each other. Sir, specifically you. It's a joy to see you share such kind words about her. You made me feel like she completes you. Wonderful!'

The couple smiled at each other with love.

The fairy added, 'And because of the devotion you have for each other, the genuine love and loyalty that you show towards each other, the aura around you helped release me from captivity inside this locket. Thank you for that. I can fulfil any desire of yours. Please make a wish.'

The couple were amazed by what was in the offing. They wondered if there could have been a more memorable gift on their wedding anniversary.

Excited, the woman looked at her husband. 'Ask for what you want to,' he said.

Looking for words, she said, 'Please can I travel to the four corners of the world with my husband and enjoy life even more?'

'Certainly,' the fairy smiled at the wife.

The wife continued, '. . . even more . . . with greater dedication and devotion to each other.'

The fairy confirmed, 'Certainly. Your desire is granted.'

The husband was now in deep thought about his wish. What could he ask that would take their happiness to a different level and they could derive even greater joy and pleasure from life?

The fairy then turned to the man and asked, 'May I know what you desire?'

The husband said, 'I concur with my wife but I have one extra desire.'

'Certainly,' the fairy assured him, 'Please tell me what it is.'

'That my wife should be thirty years younger than me. That way, I can enjoy the experience much more.'

The husband smiled at the wife, who was curious to see what the fairy would do.

At that point, the fairy looked at the wife and they exchanged glances. Then, the very next moment, the husband became ninety-five-year-old!

'I've fulfilled your desire,' the fairy reaffirmed. 'While your wife remains sixty-five years old, you are now ninety-five years old.'

In the Bhagavad Gita (16.11), Lord Krishna says,

cintām aparimeyāṁ ca
pralayāntām upāśritāḥ
kāmopabhoga-paramā
etāvad iti niścitāḥ

A conditioned soul goes through an endless cycle of anxieties. Why? Because of uncontrolled desires. People tend to think that circumstances and situations should follow their desires but no, it doesn't happen that way all the time.

They may manifest themselves at times but at other times, situations in life are beyond our control. Rather, we should attempt to control our desires and understand that real fulfilment does not depend on how many desires we fulfil but on how many desires we are able to control and eliminate. Therefore, the human form of life is meant for controlling and sublimating our desires so that with all the positive desires we can make a difference in the lives of others and our own.

There is a well-known adage: 'Unfulfilled lust develops anger and fulfilled lust leads to greed.'

The Sanskrit term for greed is lobha, which comes from the root word 'lubha' (to desire or covet) + 'ghan'.

Mahatma Gandhi once remarked famously, 'The world has enough for everyone's needs, but not enough for everyone's greed.'

Greed for the sake of success results in the dwindling of:

- **Spiritual Strength:** Because one is materially focused on piling up more and more due to unending desires, the mind becomes boxed in the quest for accumulating more, losing the real purpose of life. The spiritual dimension loses its relevance and it becomes a case of fuelling the car but not feeding the driver.

- **Austerity:** Austerity means to voluntarily accept some physical inconveniences for spiritual advancement. Whatever we wish to achieve involves some effort but effort does not necessarily imply drudgery. As we learn the transcendental art of dedicating our lives to Lord Krishna's service, an apparent hardship or problem can become a joy or a labour of love. We don't need to go looking for difficulty. We'll get it naturally, by our karma, just as we get joy. But austerity means performing our service to Krishna despite any inconvenience that might come along. Austerity is performed in speech too: speaking words that are truthful, pleasing, beneficial and not agitating to others, and also in regularly reciting Vedic literature. Austerity helps us take charge of life without remaining overtly subservient to the mind. It facilitates mind control.

- **Reputation:** Lack of contentment makes one lustful and agitates the mind. An agitated mind makes one restless and one's speech uncongenial and choice of words pungent. Such a demeanour is not welcoming and portrays one in a bad light. Further, ostentatious displays of one's greed or the exhibition of wanting to accumulate more certainly impacts one's likeability and tarnishes one's reputation in society.

- **Knowledge:** As one continues accumulating more and more, false pride surmounts and one loses the humility to learn. An 'I-know-it-all' or 'I-don't-need-to-know-more' mindset sets in. This leads to ignorance and the person loses the knowledge to lead a purposeful life.

Hunger and thirst can be satisfied by eating, Anger can be satisfied by chastisement and its reaction but even if a greedy person has conquered all the directions of the world and enjoyed everything in the world, still he will not be satisfied. That's the unending quest of greed. Just as a person wearing shoes on his feet can walk on pebbles and thorns without danger, a self-satisfied person feels happiness everywhere and is oblivious to the distress of the pebbles and thorns of various circumstances of this world.

SIXTEEN

Handle People with Care

Human Quality: Compassion

An octogenarian, with the help of her walking stick, went to a bank to withdraw money.

She walked up to the teller and politely told her, 'Madam, I would like to withdraw $500 from my account. Please can you help me?'

The teller retorted, 'There is an ATM outside for this. You may go there.' Right away, the teller looked past her and announced in a loud voice, 'Next customer please.'

'Madam, but . . . ' the old woman sought her help, 'I don't know to operate an ATM and hence I am here to get your help.'

'Don't you understand?' the teller snapped. 'For withdrawals less than $5000 you need to go to the ATM.'

Upset, the old woman shot back, 'Well, currently I want this money from the bank. I can't operate the ATM. I have come to you for help. Please be polite and help me.'

Surprised by the old woman's rejoinder, the teller replied, 'No amount less than $5000 here. Please make way for others.'

In a loud voice, the old woman announced, 'Okay. In that case, I want to withdraw all the money in my account. I don't want any dealings with a bank that is rude to customers and insensitive to their physical conditions and cognitive abilities.'

That shook the teller. In a bid to respond, she looked up the old woman's bank account details. One look at the computer in front of her left her astonished and she exclaimed, '$3.5 billion!'

Yes! That was the old woman's bank balance.

Taken aback, the teller replied politely, 'My God! Madam, you seem to have $3.5 billion in your account.'

'That's right. Please withdraw everything for me.'

'Madam, sorry that's not possible right now.'

'Do one thing,' the old woman said, 'help me withdraw $3,00,000.'

'Sure, I'll do that,' the teller responded, relieved. Immediately, she released $3,00,000 and handed over the cash to the old woman.

The old woman took $3,00,000, placed $500 in her handbag and returned the remaining amount saying, 'Please deposit this money back into my account.'

That shook the teller. She never expected the old woman to behave so cleverly.

Often, we get stuck to the rules without understanding whom we are dealing with. Therefore, the first principle is that we should consider each and every individual not on the basis of how they appear externally but on a certain value each person has intrinsically.

Lord Chaitanya Mahaprabhu says in the Sikṣāstakam:

> *tṛṇād api sunīcena*
> *taror api sahiṣṇunā*
> *amāninā mānadena*
> *kīrtanīyaḥ sadā hariḥ*

We must remain humbler than a blade of grass and more tolerant than a tree, ready to offer all respects to others but expecting none in return.

To cultivate such a divine attitude, we should not judge people externally but we should give others respect because they are a spirit soul, and a part and parcel of the Supreme Lord. They individually have a propensity to serve and love the Supreme Lord as well as all the entities connected to Him. Therefore, just because every soul is connected to the Supreme, they are worthy of respect, irrespective of what the external facade appears to be.

Let's discuss how we can maintain a balanced perspective in the midst of a conflicting situation. If we take a five-pronged approach to analysing the situation through the 'lenses' mentioned below, we can remain balanced.

- **Tolerance:** Avoid reacting immediately and exercise patience. In a conflict situation, there can be a tendency to react instantly or, as they say, have a knee-jerk reaction. The subconscious intent is towards one-upmanship that stems from the ego getting hurt. It's important to understand that it's not about who wins the conflict or about scoring brownie points but it's about facilitating an atmosphere of camaraderie and putting the other person at ease. To foster long-lasting relationships, it's better to lose first and win people forever than to win first and lose people forever. That attitude comes with maturity. Maturity is about balancing boldness and sensitivity, it's about balancing courage and being considerate.

- **Circumstance:** Try to understand the background of events. It is said, 'if content is king, context is God'. Delving into the context of situations is key to building a holistic understanding and then framing responses accordingly. Often, one can respond on the face value of a conversation without understanding the undercurrents at play and context as to why a certain person behaves in a certain way in a certain situation.

- **Acceptance:** Understand that differences are entirely natural. 'All fingers are not the same' goes a famous Persian expression. This implies that differences in people are natural. In fact, differences exist within us. We are not the same people that we were in the past. We evolve with time as we go through the process called life. New experiences stimulate us, interactions with people from other cultures inspire us and moving out of our comfort zones stirs us. Hence, it's important that we acknowledge and accept differences and do not expect that people respond to us the way we expect them to, as if they are our programmed bots.

- **Importance:** Put the conflict in perspective and see the bigger picture. They say, 'Do not miss the woods for the trees', implying the need to look at the bigger picture and not get lost in the specifics. In the same way, relationships are built over time, spanning multiple dealings, interactions, conversations, partnerships and discussions. A misunderstanding here and there in one dealing or partnership should not derail the larger purpose of building a robust relationship.

- **Transcendence:** The real victory is to progress, not to win. Fundamentally, our life should be led by a purpose. Our long-term aspirations, short-term goals and day-to-day pursuits should be anchored around this purpose and align with each other. Life should be viewed as a race that is to be won at all times. It's best seen as a journey where we make constant progress, learn on the way and develop ourselves to be better human beings each day.

SEVENTEEN

Resolving Conflict

Human Quality: Collaboration

An old man had three sons and seventeen camels. He died one day due to a cardiac arrest. Later, when the sons read his will, they discovered the following instructions: The eldest son was to be given one-half of the total camels, the second son to be given one-third and the youngest son to be given one-ninth of the camels.

Having read the instructions, the sons were bewildered. They wondered how they would divide seventeen camels into one-half, one-third and one-ninth. Confused, they sat on it for a day.

The next day, the eldest son proposed: 'Whenever we are in doubt or in need of help, we should turn to a saintly person. One who is sagacious and will help us sail through the tough times.'

The younger brothers nodded and followed the words of their eldest brother. Right away, they approached their family guru and presented their predicament before him. The saint thought for a while and announced that he had identified the solution to their problem.

The brothers felt relieved and eagerly looked forward to what the saint was going to say.

The saint began, 'Well, here is one camel from my side. I shall add this camel to the lot that you have. That makes it a total of eighteen camels. Now, let's divide.'

Looking at the eldest son, he said, 'Eighteen divided by two. Please take nine camels.'

Drawing the attention of the second son, he said, 'Eighteen divided by three. Please take six camels.'

Pointing to the youngest son, he concluded, 'Eighteen divided by nine. Please take two camels.'

'Now,' he added, pointing to all three of them, 'nine plus six plus two. That's seventeen camels. There will be one camel left. That's the one that I added. Let me take that back.'

The sons were amazed by how the saint had settled the issue effortlessly and amicably.

What appeared to be an impossible task actually became possible when everybody was open to reaching a common ground. Sometimes, differences of opinion run so deep and so intense that the parties in conflict feel that a resolution is not possible. But the point is that all kinds of peace-making efforts and negotiation efforts will only be successful when the parties are open and aligned to the idea that a solution can indeed be arrived at. Only when there is a will, all kinds of skills can add value.

In the *Srimad Bhagavatam* (8.8.38), it is said,

> *mithaḥ kalir abhūt teṣāṁ*
> *tad-arthe tarṣa-cetasām*
> *ahaṁ pūrvam ahaṁ pūrvaṁ*
> *na tvaṁ na tvam iti prabho*

This is in the context of the samudra manthan lila. During the churning process by the devatas and the demons, and as the pot of nectar rose above, both parties clashed and began fighting to stake claim over the pot: 'Not you, not you, but me.' The Supreme Lord intervened and set things right. Therefore, if we decide to reach a common ground, it can only be on the basis of willingness to set aside false ego and find that eighteenth camel, as illustrated in the story above. When that eighteenth camel was added, we observed how an amicable settlement emerged and a common ground was established. When we are in a situation of conflict, we should earnestly apply our mind and intelligence to try and figure out how we can find that common ground, that eighteenth camel, through which all issues can be amicably resolved.

The *Srimad Bhagavatam* declares: 'If all our desires in life are like an ocean, the human body is like a boat endowed with the power to cross over.' This ocean of desires should be guided by the captain (the Spiritual Master or Guru), taking the help of the sails in the form of holy scriptures and leveraging the winds of favourable circumstances. The wisdom of the wise certainly helps us become better sailors to navigate the ship better during periods of unexpected and prolonged storms in life.

In life, we should choose the right leader to guide us and help us handle conflicting situations in life ably.

An able leader must:

- **Connect with Divinity:** Leaders must not think that they are the supreme being who have a team to control. Rather, they should see themselves as servants of God who have been given the opportunity to serve the people as leaders. In that frame of mind, if a leader were to operate, he/she would serve the team to the best of his/her abilities and lead with care. In such a mindset, with God at the centre, the leader leads on His behalf and connects with people as a part and parcel of God's creation.

- **Care with Humanity:** Compassion is the driver of their behaviour. As the well-known song of Narsinh Mehta goes,

> *vaiṣṇava jana to tene kahiye*
> *je pīḍa parāyī jāṇe re*
> *para duḥkhe upakāra kare to ye*
> *mana abhimāna na āṇe re*

They truly live this as they are able to feel the pain of others, help those who are in misery but never let self-conceit enter their mind.

- **Communicate with Clarity:** Leaders are clear in terms of what they are setting out for and lead the team with that level of clarity. Communication skills are a differentiator that separate ordinary leaders from able leaders.
- **Cope with Diversity:** They recognize natural differences that exist in people and embrace diversity. Able leaders make no discrimination between people and provide equal opportunities for one and all. They not only practise vasudhaiva kutumbakam (the world is one family) but instil the same in their team members to promote universal brotherhood.

- **Conquer with Agility:** Able leaders understand the potential of individual team members as they connect with them individually and with humanity. Well aware of the unique strengths as well as the development areas of individual team members, they are adept in organizing the team for tasks. Devoid of any superiority complex, they remain approachable and lead with agility.

EIGHTEEN

Lucky or Unlucky

Human Quality: Gratitude

A construction supervisor was once overseeing a project in the middle of the city in Mumbai. With high-rise buildings towering into the sky and three-tier transport around the area, including ships in the sea, the flyovers, the metro rail to help navigate the buzzing traffic, it was the chaos of the city manifesting in those surroundings. Add to that, the construction work: creaking of metal, scraping of wooden logs and grinding of other materials made hearing a strenuous activity.

The supervisor was working on the second floor of that building. He wanted to draw the attention of a worker on the ground floor urgently. He tried shouting his name out loud but the worker didn't respond. The supervisor made different sounds, but nothing quite changed the result. The ambient noise made communication impossible there. The supervisor wondered what best he could do and then thought of an idea.

He took out two currency notes in the denomination of Rs 100, crushed them hard into a paper ball and aimed it at the worker's back. The paper ball ricocheted and fell down next to the worker's legs. When the worker noticed the Rs 100 paper ball, unfazed, he quietly picked it up, uncrumpled it to discover two such notes and put them into his pocket. Then, he continued with his work. Bemused, the supervisor thought maybe the denomination was small. So, he tried the same approach but with Rs 500 notes. The worker's response was the same.

The supervisor got irritated and had to think of something more impactful so as to avoid climbing down two floors. Now, he thought of another trick.

He picked up a small stone lying nearby, aimed and threw it at the worker. That small stone hit the helmet of the worker and made a sound. Immediately, the worker looked up and shouted, 'Who's that throwing stones at me?'

The supervisor told him he had done so and why. Then he communicated his message.

Life is also like that. When we are blessed with fortunes and necessities in life by the grace of God, we only keep collecting them, amassing them, using them and sometimes even abusing them without even thinking of looking up and thanking Him with gratitude. However, when there is a problem in life, we immediately get agitated, look up and complain right away, 'How can you do this to me?'

Therefore, it is described in the *Srimad Bhagavatam* (3.19.36),

tam sukhārādhyam ṛjubhir
ananya-śaraṇair nṛbhiḥ
kṛtajñaḥ ko na seveta
durārādhyam asādhubhiḥ

The Supreme Lord confirms that He can be approached with great simplicity and a heart filled with gratitude and if one does not have the simplicity and gratitude, it is practically impossible to experience and express one's devotion.

Gratitude begins with us appreciating the many gifts we receive: the air to breathe, the water to drink, the succulent vegetables, nutritious rich grains, tasty milk, etc., to eat and drink, and all kinds of facilities and faculties with respect to our body, mind, intelligence and senses. It's hard to fathom the magnanimity of the Supreme Lord. He supplies these extraordinary facilities graciously and it's worth to note that only He can supply them all. Despite His exclusivity, what He looks forward to is our love and nothing else in return. There are multiple means to express gratitude to God. In this day and age, the best method is the chanting of the name of God. The Hare Krishna maha mantra is subscribed for this age of kali yuga: Hare Krishna, Hare Krishna, Krishna Krishna, Hare Hare, Hare Rama, Hare Rama, Rama Rama, Hare Hare.

As we deliberate on this topic of gratitude, here are simple ways by which we can genuinely express gratitude, not just to God but to anyone who makes a positive impact on us.

- **Remembering the Person(s) Who Helped Us:** A grateful heart remembers the people who have helped us become who we are. These could be parents, siblings, teachers, friends and seniors, to name a few. It's not always possible that they are near us for us to express our gratitude, but a thoughtful remembrance of people purifies us. In the busy lives that we lead, a telephone call to them enquiring about them is a manifestation of gratitude.

- **Remembering the Exact Details of the Nature of How They Helped Us:** It's certainly good to remember the people who helped us. But delving deeper and remembering the specifics of their kind help lent when it mattered most takes our gratitude to the next level. Love lies in attention to details. As we think deeper about their deeds, the heart immerses itself in the gesture and purifies us even further for a stream of gratitude to flow, wiping away any hard feelings inadvertently present.

- **Contemplating How Their Help Has Affected Us and Transformed Our Life Positively:** Building on the point above, it's important to think through how a certain kind gesture transformed us at that point in time in life. This could be an elder sibling teaching us math in childhood or it could be an uncle lending balance as we learnt cycling. Often, we take certain gifts for granted. But there are a lot of children who don't have the gift of an elder sibling or an uncle showering such love.

- **Reflecting on How We May Have Struggled and Suffered in the Absence of Such Timely Intervention:** When we look around us to find orphans struggling in the absence of caretakers or when our financially struggling family is unable to provide the kind of life that was a necessity for us, our heart should melt in gratitude as it was such experiences that helped shape who we are. As they say, numerous drops make an ocean. It's such numerous kind acts that make for us the fine experience called life.

- **Reciting a Silent Prayer for Their Well-being:** Going one step above just expressing gratitude by saying sincere thanks would be to say a prayer for their well-being. The supreme truth is that each one of us are part and parcels of God and that it is He who provides the strength to living beings and even empowers people when they want to help someone. A sincere prayer to God could be to request Him to shower His choicest blessings upon the kind soul that helped and continue to empower that individual to commit to making such a positive difference in the lives of people.

- **Reciprocating with an Appropriate Gesture of Words and Action at the Earliest Opportunity:** The best means to complete the circle of gratitude is to reciprocate in words and, when possible, to return the help by doing our best in the situation to help them when required. There isn't a best time to help people. The helping gesture makes that instant of time auspicious.

NINETEEN

Honesty Wins

Human Quality: Integrity

There was once a king who did not have a successor. As the seventh-generation ruler, he was disappointed that such a rich legacy would not have an heir from the family. He consulted his astrologer and priests to seek advice. Despite performing various pujas, begetting a child remained elusive. He accepted his reality and decided to leave the kingdom to the best person there. He was keen that someone honest, caring and trustworthy should succeed him. The king discussed this with the prime minister and set in motion the process for the selection of a successor without revealing the intent behind this exercise.

The king was a botany aficionado and wanted to roll out an activity on those lines. He called all the children in the kingdom and distributed among them all a small pot. There was mud in that pot. Along with the pot, he gave them a seed and said, 'Please take care of this seed in such a way that proves to me after one year how well you cared for it. I would like to see how well the plant grows.'

All the children went away and every month they would come and report the progress of their plant's growth to the prime minister. A year passed and all the children assembled again, each one trying to show off how their plant had grown taller and wider than all the other plants. The prime minister was elated with the response and the way the children had participated in the competition. The king and the minister were going through each and every pot. Finally, they stopped in front of one boy's plant. They were astonished to find that the boy's pot had mud but there was no trace of a plant in it.

The king looked at this boy and said, 'Everyone has come with their pots filled with plants. I am very impressed with them.'

The boy smiled, listening to the king intently.

'But,' the king continued, 'how is it that your pot is empty? What happened? Where are the plants? Where is the flower from your seed?'

The boy replied, 'My dear king, I have been sincerely and diligently watering and fertilizing this soil, which contains the seed you gave us last year. Believe me, in spite of all my efforts, I have not been able to achieve any success.'

Beaming, the king listened to the boy.

'The seed simply refused to germinate,' the boy added, 'Please help me. What should I do?'

Thrilled, the king lifted the boy in his arms and patted him on the back. He announced, 'This child will become the king after me. From today, I will take care of him, nurture him and give him the best opportunities to learn and grow.'

Everyone was shocked. No one knew that this was an exercise to select the king's successor.

There were whispers all around.

'What's going on with the king?'

'Has the king gone mad?'

'That's such a lucky boy.'

'This child could not even grow a small plant. His entire pot is empty; why him?'

'What a life he will have.'

'My son is not as gifted.'

'My son missed by a whisker; but how come this boy, who couldn't even grow a plant, won?'

'Of all the children, why him?'

'How can he be declared the king?'

The prime minister walked up to the king and murmured, 'Respected king, I was aware of the intent of this exercise but what I don't understand is why this boy.'

'I'll address that too,' the king replied with a smile.

He then addressed the crowd, 'Actually, I had distributed seeds that were roasted. You all know that roasted seeds cannot germinate. Therefore, I wanted to simply test the honesty and integrity of not just the children but the parents as well.'

That shocked the audience and there were murmurs of repentance.

'I must say that I am quite disappointed with the state of honesty in this kingdom but I am glad that one boy and his family upheld the sacred values of honesty and integrity.'

It is said in the *Srimad Bhagavatam* (10.2.26),

satya-vrataṁ satya-paraṁ tri-satyaṁ
satyasya yoniṁ nihitaṁ ca satye
satyasya satyam ṛta-satya-netraṁ
satyātmakaṁ tvāṁ śaraṇaṁ prapannāḥ

It is described herein that the Supreme Personality of Godhead is satya (truth). In every aspect of the entire creation, past, present and future, He remains the truth. And, therefore, the soul by nature is eternally part and parcel of the Supreme Soul and truthfulness is the core total element of every soul. Unless and until we experience that truthfulness within, we cannot express that truthfulness. With this core principle, we should strive to follow the spiritual principles diligently and transform our heart and our consciousness on the foundation of truthfulness.

One human quality in which truth manifests in full is integrity. My spiritual master, H.H. Radhanath Swami, says, 'Integrity means to be honest, to be truthful and to make great sacrifices for the welfare of others. Integrity is to maintain our ideals and our values even in the face of temptation and fear. If one compromises integrity for the cheap thrill of this world, one is going to suffer miserably. Winning the game of life means to maintain our integrity.'

Integrity as a trait is very important for our holistic well-being, physically, mentally and spiritually.

- **Integrity Helps Align Our Action with Our Values:**
  Integrity is also described as 'do what you say'. If we lead

a life based on integrity, we perform our actions in line with our values, which act as a fulcrum of our thoughts. A person with integrity never manipulates or misleads people with the gift of the gab.

- **Integrity Speaks of the Entire Character of the Person:** Integrity is compromised if there is inconsistency. In today's world, where we partner with people globally on projects and assignments at work so easily, often, we are not physically connected. More so now, in the COVID-affected world, remote working is the new normal. In such a situation, people with a proven track record of integrity score over others as they are seen as reliable. Leaders hand over projects and empower such people to lead and grow in the system.

- **Integrity Maintains Peace of Mind Within:** When we say that one maintains integrity, one is true to conscience. There is no wordplay management or separate vigil on the choice of words required. Often, when people dabble in manipulation or lies, they get confused wondering what has been said to whom and what needs to be done to set things right. However, if one follows the path of truth, there is peace within.

TWENTY

Never Give Up

Human Quality: Perseverance

In the country of Armenia, a couple, Lana and Daniel, had a son, Arman.

One morning, they sent Arman to school as usual. It seemed a regular day until that afternoon. As the day progressed, an earthquake shook the city. The earthquake had a very high magnitude on the Richter scale and its epicentre was in the area where Arman's school was located. The surrounding areas in the city were not affected but there was massive devastation within a 4-km radius around Arman's school. Just like other tall buildings, the school building too had collapsed at many places.

Arman's father, Daniel, went running to the school. To his shock, he found that the entire school building was nothing but a mass of debris. It appeared that practically no one had survived. People from nearby localities thronged the area but no one moved an inch—they just watched the ghastly devastation before their eyes.

'Why are you all doing nothing?' Daniel shouted at the crowd as he reached the school premises.

'What is there to do here?' one man shouted back.

Without wasting any time arguing with the people there, Daniel walked into a pile of debris and started removing one brick after the other and throwing away pieces of metal that had fallen there.

'What are you trying to do?' one man asked loudly.

'I'm trying to save my son,' Daniel cried.

'That's impossible,' the man said. 'Whoever was here, they have all been crushed under the weight of this debris.'

'No, I must try to save my son,' Daniel insisted.

He persisted. An hour passed, then two, three, four, eight, twelve. People came and went. The sun set. But Daniel persisted in his efforts despite the faint street light. Against all odds, fourteen hours later, Daniel kept moving one piece of debris after another, dislodging pieces of stone, wood and metal. Finally, he heard the divine sound he had been looking forward to hearing: 'Papa.'

In inexplicable delight, Daniel cried, 'Hey Arman, Is that you?'

'Yes,' the child sobbed.

'Come out. I have created a small opening here,' Daniel directed Arman. 'You can come out of this.'

'Dad,' Arman said, 'I know for sure that you will save me. But before that, I have my friends here. I want you to save them first.'

'For sure, kiddo,' Daniel shouted in deep ecstasy, thrilled at the thought of finally reuniting with his son. All his efforts seemed to be bearing fruit.

Daniel made his way through that opening. As he made the opening bigger, he discovered that many children were alive because the debris had fallen on a piece of large metal that was still intact. That metal had protected the children from getting crushed. Fourteen children were saved that day, thanks to the efforts of one hopeful father who refused to give up. Of course, his son, Arman was saved as well.

And therefore, in the Bhagavad Gita (2.47), Krishna says,

karmaṇy evādhikāras te
mā phaleṣu kadācana
mā karma-phala-hetur bhūr
mā te saṅgo 'stv akarmaṇi

Each one of us has a right to perform our duty and we should not be attached to the results. If we simply strive to operate in life based on this fundamental principle, we save ourselves from a lot of anxiety. Often times, we are attached to the fruits of the activity. For example, in school, we studied hard with an aim to score high grades. If we only enjoyed the process of learning and committed ourselves to the process with dedication, we wouldn't have felt tense on the day of the exam. This anxiety stems from our thought process that everything is in our control. Actually it is not! Getting clarity on the syllabus, studying smart, practicing hard, referring to the previous years' question papers diligently and entering the exam hall with a positive mindset are in our control. However, the nature of the question paper and the problems set are beyond our control. This is a simple example and we can extrapolate this to many situations in life. The best approach always is to 'do your best and leave the rest to God'.

In the journey towards our life's goals, we must persevere and avoid being tricked in the following five ways:

- **Complacency:** They say that 'familiarity breeds contempt'. As an extrapolation to that, when we revisit a situation in life that appears to give us a feeling of déjà vu, there is a tendency to be complacent as we tell ourselves, 'I've seen it and done it'. It's an involuntary thought mechanism that is rooted in the mind. The root of this attitude lies in the pride that develops with success. As a result, we don't give as much importance to the activity or pay attention to details. This carelessness can make us fail even in tasks that we should have otherwise sailed through smoothly. The tale of the hare and the tortoise is a classic example of this trait. The learning is that we should remain vigilant and cautious.

- **Isolation:** Sometimes, people tend to think that they are better off alone as that gives them more space and independence. Yes, there are certain activities where this is applicable and can be leveraged to their advantage. However, one shouldn't isolate oneself because of one's unwillingness to collaborate. Of course, this is a mindset problem. Sometimes, when the same people do not have a choice but work in a team it leads to arguments, misunderstandings, personality differences and cultural barriers. Such incidents distance them from potentially likeminded souls and such loneliness may compromise their strength and protection in life. As they say, 'united we stand, divided we fall'.

- **Hopelessness:** The story we read above is a prime example of how Daniel never lost hope. He showed great character and remained relentless in his pursuit to save his son. In the end, he saved not just his son but a host of other children as well.

  Like Daniel, every aspirant is confronted with the gap between the real (of where they are) and the ideal (of where they would like to be) state. Depending on the mindset of the person, this gap can tend to:

  o **Be Uncomfortable:** That they haven't been able to make it to where they want to be makes them feel uncomfortable. They just can't cope with reality (most times) that they fall short of expectations. That keeps them mentally disturbed and uncomfortable with accepting who they are.

  o **Create Guilt:** Here it becomes a question of capability and they feel guilty for not getting there yet. What they fail to realize is that with consistent efforts and dutifully approaching their target, they can accomplish it one day. Such people remain stuck in the mode of ignorance.

  o **Creates Frustration:** There is a sense of uneasiness that permeates the minds of people sometimes. That they are stuck in the mode of passion to accomplish what they want and that too instantly, by their whims and fancies, they just can't tolerate the current situation they are in. There is a feeling of uneasiness in the mind and that makes them frustrated. This frustration blocks their mind from operating normally. Because their mind is surcharged with anger and frustration, they are unable to focus on the end goal clearly.

- **Diversion:** The problem is outside. We get diverted from our goal and focus on people, places and situations surrounding us. We end up being compulsively busy, addressing the externals, diverting ourselves from the real goal. If we are averse to change and hope that the world outside will change, we are living in denial. It's important to understand that we need to adapt according to the world around us and that the world will not adapt according to us.

- **Pride:** Pride is straightforward. People relate to it as an impediment and one that can come in the way of success. Let me share a simple but powerful example. While playing snakes and ladders, one may reach the ninety-nineth square quickly but still get bitten by the snake and be forced to start from the bottom. When we gain name, fame, appreciation and success, we feel that our journey is complete. Definitely not! The snake of pride bites us and eats us from within. Unless internal purity develops and manifests in the core of the heart, we continue to remain vulnerable.

TWENTY-ONE

Guru Bhakti

Human Quality: Devotion

There was once a boy who was keen to learn the Vedas. He approached a saint in a hermitage far away from his village. As the saint enquired about him, the boy shared that he had walked all the way from a far-off village where there was no scope for formal education. He expressed his desire to study under a learned saint.

The saint continued to look at the boy and didn't speak a word.

'Please teach me the Vedas,' the boy pleaded.

The saint was pleased with the boy's earnestness and said, 'Well, it takes at least twelve years to learn the Vedas. They are very difficult.'

'Guruji,' the boy affirmed, 'I'm willing to learn under your guidance.'

The guru accepted him and his formal education commenced. The ashram education went on for twelve years and the guru inculcated in the boy the fundamentals of Vedic education. He also taught the boy the philosophy expounded in the Vedas, the Upanishads, the Puranas and the Itihasas.

For twelve years, the student studied diligently. Then, it was time for his graduation.

That day, the guru, after congratulating all the students, explained, 'We have a very different type of graduation here. Students should stand under this tree and recite all the important philosophical understanding and verses that they have absorbed. If there is any mistake in your recitation, the leaves of the tree will start falling. The number of leaves that fall off indicate the number of mistakes that you make.'

The boy who had come from the far-off village went first.

He stood under the tree and started meditating on the deities of knowledge to remove all obstacles from his path, to begin with. As he meditated on those deities sincerely, all the leaves fell.

Flummoxed, he approached the guru and said, 'Well, I have not even started my recitation and all the leaves have already fallen.'

'Well, what did you meditate upon?' the guru asked.

'All I did was to remember the deities. And as soon as I remembered the deities and started invoking the various prayers and the deities' names, the leaves fell off.'

With a smile, the guru said, 'Well, you forgot a very important prayer. Before remembering the deities, you should have remembered your gurus—those who taught you all of this knowledge.'

In the Vedic tradition, on the path of perfection in spiritual life, it's essential to receive guidance from a guru, a spiritual master or guide, because we can't directly or immediately approach God on our own.

For example, if we want to meet the President or Prime Minister, we are not allowed to knock on their door and get an audience. We either need to make an appointment with their secretary or get an introduction from a mutual friend. It is applicable even in the case of God, the foremost person and, in fact, the cause of this creation. Each one of us has a direct relationship with God because we are His children but realizing and acting in that direct relationship is possible after we've become pure, which is a process. A spiritual master is the guide who selflessly trains and guides us in reviving our relationship with God and the guru is always willing to help us in difficult times. Showing gratitude to him, who shows us the way to God, is the most essential quality of a sincere heart.

We can recognize a genuine spiritual master by the following qualities. Such a master:

- is well-versed in Vedic scriptures and follows their principles
- identifies as the humble servant of God and never claims to be God
- acts with full control of his/her senses and never falls under their control
- is impeccable in his/her moral character
- is fully dedicated to serving God, at all times, with body, mind and words
- follows a guru who belongs to a genuine line of gurus, a line that extends all the way back to Krishna, the original spiritual master of everyone

When we follow strictly the guidance of such a spiritual master, our success in spiritual life is guaranteed.

In the Bhagavad Gita (4.34), Krishna says,

tad viddhi praṇipātena
paripraśnena sevayā
upadekṣyanti te jñānaṁ
jñāninas tattva-darśinaḥ

Just try to learn the truth by approaching a spiritual master. Inquire from him submissively and render service unto him. The self-realized souls can impart knowledge unto you because they have seen the truth.

In this verse, both following someone blindly and absurd inquiries are condemned. Not only should one inquire submissively from the spiritual master, but one must also get a clear understanding from him, in submission and service, and in making inquiries. A bona fide spiritual master is, by nature, very kind towards the disciple. Therefore, when the student is submissive and is always ready to render service, the reciprocation of knowledge and inquiries becomes perfect.

It is the spiritual master who shows us the path to Krishna. Hence, the first respects are reserved for the spiritual master. That indeed is a sign of gratitude. Expression of profuse gratitude pleases Krishna, the supreme object of pleasure.

The importance of gratitude of heart is corroborated in the *Srimad Bhagavatam* (3.19.36),

tam sukhārādhyam ṛjubhir
ananya-śaraṇair nṛbhiḥ
kṛtajñaḥ ko na seveta
durārādhyam asādhubhiḥ

To offer devotional service to Krishna requires the foundation of gratitude. And by having gratitude in one's life, it becomes very easy to please and serve Krishna. When we please the guru, we please Krishna, and when we please Krishna, we please the guru.

TWENTY-TWO

The Search for Water

Human Quality: Compassion

A man was once walking through the desert. It was a sunny afternoon and very humid. The tent where he was staying was at quite a distance. Feeling weak, thirsty and faint, he started looking for water. After he dragged himself a few paces forward, he couldn't walk any more. He began to crawl on the sand and started to cry for help, hoping there was someone inhabiting that lonely desert.

He had crawled for a few metres when he spotted at a distance a shelter that looked like a hut. He tried to focus his eyes to get a better view of the hut and crawled forward. Once he confirmed that it was indeed a hut, he regained some energy and crawled faster. He even managed to raise himself to jump a few more metres forward. He walked inside the hut ecstatically. He had great hope of finding someone inside the hut to help him quench his thirst. If not, he was hoping against hope for some water inside the hut at least.

As he entered the hut, he felt relieved to find a handpump in the corner. On seeing the handpump, he looked up instantly, thanked God and said a prayer. Enthused, he dragged himself and touched the handpump like a customer caressing a newly purchased gold ornament. With great anticipation, he began pumping it. There was a gurgling sound but no water. Still, he didn't lose faith. He applied whatever energy he had into this activity. Despite his best efforts, there was no water. About to lose hope, he looked around in search of help. Suddenly, he noticed a bottle of water lying on the side. He picked it up immediately because it was exactly what he was looking for—the elixir of his life then, water.

As he held the bottle of water, he noticed that it was corked. There was a small message on the bottle too. It said, 'First, please pour this water at the base of the handpump so that water comes out. Two, please make sure that when the water comes out, you refill this bottle and keep it back the way you found it.'

Now, he was caught in a dilemma. Here was an opportunity for him to drink that bottle of water and quench his thirst directly but if he did as the message instructed him to do, he would have to let go of the bottle of water with the hope that water could be flushed out from the pump. He wondered if he should just help himself or help others too. He introspected despite his current state: physically weak and mentally disturbed. He asked himself whether he should empathize with someone else who could be in a similar state of mind at some point in the future or just gulp the water and leave the place. Doubts crept into his mind.

He thought to himself, 'If I pour this entire one litre of water at the base of the pump, what if I don't get the water back? Who knows, the pump may be malfunctioning. Then, I will die of thirst.' On the flip side, he wondered, 'Should it work fine, then I can pump more than a litre of water and also help someone else.'

Confused, he said a prayer to God. Finally, he decided to take a leap of faith and follow the instructions on the bottle. He opened the bottle and poured the water at the base of the pump. With whatever energy he had in him, he began pumping. The more he pumped, the louder the gurgling sound, just like before. He kept faith and pumped harder; the gurgling grew louder. Within moments, water came gushing out of the pump. He was jubilant and thanked the Almighty.

He lapped up the water and drank it to his heart's content. As instructed, he filled the bottle of water to the brim and corked it. Just as he was about to leave, he thought of doing something special. He took out a pen from his pocket and added a footnote to the instructions: 'This message is bona fide. It does work and I am convinced.'

Lord Krishna says in the Bhagavad Gita (17.20),

dātavyam iti yad dānaṁ
dīyate 'nupakāriṇe
deśe kāle ca pātre ca
tad dānaṁ sāttvikaṁ smṛtam

Human life is meant to be shared with others, to give to others what we have. If we remain simply concerned with our own selfish interests and neglect the interests, needs and concerns of others, very soon that selfishness will engulf us to keep us perpetual thirsty. We should always seek to utilize whatever has been given to us to the best of our ability and remember always to share and give to others so that others also benefit and we experience deep satisfaction.

The Ramayana illustrates multiple examples of selfless personalities and the events when such selflessness came to the fore and demonstrated the righteous way of life:

- Although the Supreme Lord Himself, Lord Rama wholeheartedly accepted his exile. Despite not having committed any fault, he didn't protest or question the sentence. He put, above all, the need to honour the word of his father, King Dasharatha. This is a demonstrated example of why Lord Rama is also known as Maryada Purushottam. That is, He appeared to show the ideal human behaviour. He lived a life as the perfect son, the perfect disciple, the perfect husband and the perfect king. Lord Rama was extremely merciful and grateful for even the smallest of services rendered to Him. He performed as a son the funeral ceremony of Jatayu (a bird), who gave up his life to protect Mother Sita. Lord Rama was extremely pleased with Sugriva and the other monkeys for assisting Him in the war against Ravana. It is said that all the monkey soldiers who died in war came back to life due to Lord Rama's mercy. He embraced Lord Hanuman for successfully finding Mother Sita.

It is said in the *Srimad Bhagavatam* (9.11.23)

puruṣo rāma-caritaṁ
śravaṇair upadhārayan
ānṛśaṁsya-paro rājan
karma-bandhair vimucyate

That anyone who aurally receives the narrations concerning the characteristics of Lord Rama's pastimes will ultimately be freed from the disease of envy and, thus, be liberated from the bondage of fruitive activities.

Lord Rama is certainly a great inspiration for the current generation of children to imbibe the values of obedience, tolerance, selflessness and gratitude.

• Mother Sita behaved as the ideal wife when she voluntarily chose to follow Her husband in His exile. By doing this, she chose the dangers of the forest over the security of the palace. When Lord Rama made the announcement of his exile and requested Her to stay back in Ayodhya while she permitted Him to leave, Mother Sita was saddened. She was not sorry about the cancellation of Her husband's coronation nor at the demanded crowning of Bharata. But she felt angry that Lord Rama should leave her behind and go to the forest alone. She declared: 'My Lord, I can't stay for a moment in a place without you. In your absence, this Ayodhya will be a jungle to me. The forest where you stay will be my kingdom. My life runs under your shadow.' These words of response reflect Her intimacy in the relationship, tolerance and selflessness. She continues to be an inspiration for householders to get better at marital commitments.

• Right from His childhood, Lakshmana was very affectionate towards His elder brother, Lord Rama, and served Him both with body and mind. Lakshman's life is a hallmark of brotherly sacrifice. He lived His every breath for Lord Rama. Without Lord Rama asleep on the bed, Lakshman wouldn't sleep; without Lord Rama tasting the newly cooked dishes, Lakshman wouldn't contemplate eating even when served food; whenever Lord Rama went out on horseback, Lakshman would follow Him with bow and arrows to protect Him. The intent of Lakshman to always protect Him should be understood in the context of selfless service. Before someone could even think of attempting to attack Lord Rama, Lakshmana would be ready to sacrifice His life. His life should serve as an antidote to the superficial relationships that characterize today's siblings.

- Bharat's selfless service and reverence for Lord Rama is second only to Lakshman's reverence. The example of Bharata's sacrifice in resolutely refusing the kingdom meant for Lord Rama should offer a lesson on the many succession battles among children that start after the death of a wealthy parent or, at times, even before their death. Bharat was so humble and respectful that He let the footwear (paduka) of Lord Rama adorn the throne, while he remained a meek servant of His divine brother.

TWENTY-THREE

There Is Someone Smarter

Human Quality: Humility

There were four friends in high school. These four friends enjoyed playing tricks, indulging in frivolous activities and bullying other students. The bonding among the four friends and their indulgence in such activities was well known to the school authorities. The friends hated studying and exams terrified them. The math exam, even more so. Having failed in the math exam earlier that year, they wanted to escape it this time. The day of the math exam arrived and they missed it as planned.

The following day, the dean called them and asked, 'Why did you miss the exam?'

'Sir,' one friend said, 'we had gone for a friend's wedding. As we were returning from the wedding, the car's tyre burst.'

The rest of them nodded, self-pityingly.

'As we pushed the car for a while,' he added, 'we were completely exhausted.'

'And so, we couldn't appear for the exam, sir,' the second friend concurred.

'All right,' the dean said, giving hope to the friends that he seemed to have believed their story.

'Thank you so much,' the first friend said with a smile.

'We appreciated your understanding, sir,' the second friend said, while the third added, 'We are indebted to you.'

The fourth simply smiled. As they were about to leave the dean's office, he stopped them.

'Come with me,' the dean remarked, taking them to a nearby classroom.

'I will give you an opportunity to appear for an exam. This is not math,' the dean said. The friends were thrilled to hear this.

'This exam is different,' the dean added, infusing curiosity in their minds. 'The paper contains just two questions and the duration is ten minutes.'

The friends were elated and wondered if there was a better substitute for their math exam. They accepted the dean's proposal and were keen to oblige him at the earliest.

'Shall we take the exam now, sir?' the first friend asked eagerly.

'Why not? Sure,' the dean nodded. He whispered something into the ears of one of his staff members and joined as the invigilator for the exam. He made the friends sit on four chairs placed far apart and handed over the question paper.

As promised, the paper had only two questions. The first question was: 'What is your name?'

The second one was a multiple-choice question: 'Which car tyre had burst?' This was followed by four options: front right, front left, back right and back left.

That stumped the friends and they looked at each other in dismay. They apologized to the dean and confessed to their mistake.

In the Bhagavad Gita (7.7), Lord Krishna says,

> *mattaḥ parataraṁ nānyat*
> *kiñcid asti dhanañ-jaya*
> *mayi sarvam idaṁ protaṁ*
> *sūtre maṇi-gaṇā iva*

That there is no power superior to me. It is impossible for anyone to outsmart the intelligence of the Supreme Lord. Each one of us living beings are part and parcel of the Supreme Lord, Krishna. For one with propensity to cheat, they may get away with something for some time but not get away with all things at all times. In the long run, the Supreme Lord in the form of (kāla) time factor catches up with them. Therefore, we should be conscious of our behaviour, be honest to ourselves and true to conscience, come to terms with the fact that we are under the control of the Almighty, appreciate and understand the different forces that control us and how we can overcome this by engaging in the service of God always; devotional service that is.

A person who tries to cheat experiences the five effects of karma:

- **Cry:** Enslaved by unlimited desires, they constantly crave for what they desire, just like the well-known saying states, 'we get what we deserve and not what we desire'.

In the process of attaining it, they always remain anxious. And finally, as the factor of merit catches up with them and they end up on the losing side, they become dejected by the outcome. As a result, they live dissatisfied and cry for more

- **Lie:** Enraged by burning desires from within, their intelligence doesn't let them discriminate or think objectively. In constant pursuit of what they hanker for, their uncontrollable and irresistible desires force them to behave ignobly and choose immoral actions, including lying. Due to constant lying and spreading rumours, they lose credibility and reputation in society.

- **Vie:** Driven passionately by the desire to achieve something, their moral blindness makes them ruthlessly competitive. They tend to see situations in life as a race and fellow beings as competitors or, at times, enemies, depending on the intensity of the challenge that they appear to pose. In this process, these persons fail to recognize the good in others or promote learning of those noteworthy attributes in life. Rather than collaborating and nurturing shared learning, they end up creating enmity.

- **Die:** Despite the efforts and the falsehood strategy developed to accomplish their desires, they succeed occasionally but ultimately, they die. As is with all materialistic scheming, timing of the end is a mystery and they are abruptly terminated at some point in time.

- **Fie:** In the mad race that such people pursue, the world around them takes notice of them and develops a sense of disgust for their attitude to life. The paramatma present within the person remains neutral yet compassionate and concerned about the immoral activities of the person. Yet, the truth remains that this person had lost a golden opportunity for elevation of consciousness in life. Swayed by material illusion, they are bereft of opportunities for spiritual elevation in the next life.

Karma can be overcome if we tie our intelligence to the ethics revealed in our ancient wisdom.

TWENTY-FOUR

The Pot of Wit

Human Quality: Positive Thinking

A master had a very intelligent servant assist him for a long time. They respected and complemented each other as well. Suddenly, a difference of opinion arose between them on a certain issue. This led to a fight that ended with the servant leaving the master. The servant left with the warning that he would never return to the master. Agitated by the gravity of the situation, the master sent him out without any concern for his long-term service, sharp intellect and presence of mind.

A few days passed and the master began to find the going tough. Two weeks passed and he realized how indispensable the servant was. His intelligence was badly missed and that impacted the master's functioning. The master was really keen to get the servant back. The master made up his mind to apologize for his mistakes and to accept him back graciously.

He searched for the servant through word of mouth and advertisements but in vain.

The master thought hard and devised an idea. What differentiated the servant from others was his sharp intellect. The master wanted to tap into it. The town's leader was a good friend of the master and hence he reached out to him for help.

The town leader sent out a message to the local villages, 'Over the years, you have been paying taxes. No more taxes! Now, I want you all to send me a pot of wit. If you are not able to give me a pot of wit, you will have to fill a pot with gold, jewels, rubies and emeralds, and send it to me.'

The residents were bewildered. They wondered what a pot of wit meant.

The servant, who was staying in one of the local villages, got hold of a watermelon plant. The watermelon was small in size. He placed it inside the pot and made the conditions inside ideal for that watermelon to grow. Within a few weeks, the watermelon matured, covering the entire space within the pot.

He sent this pot to the town leader with the message: 'This is a pot of wit. You can try to take it out without breaking the pot.'

When the master saw this message, he beamed with joy, 'This is the village where my servant is.'

The master rushed to the village. His judgement was right. He apologized to his servant and they were reunited.

In the Bhagavad Gita (7.3), Krishna says:

> *manuṣyāṇāṁ sahasreṣu*
> *kaścid yatati siddhaye*
> *yatatām api siddhānāṁ*
> *kaścin māṁ vetti tattvataḥ*

That there are millions and millions of souls in this world but very few have the wit and the intelligence to search for the real purpose and goal in life. There are very few who are intelligent enough to try to understand that the human form of life needs to be utilized in the right way to solve the real problems of life: that is, birth, old age, disease and death. One who is able to utilize this human form of life and understand that the unique and the most special thing about this body, which is like a pot, is that only the human body is endowed with the intelligence or the wit to understand Krishna and find solutions to the cyclic problems in life.

In the Bhagavad Gita, knowledge is compared to a sword. Leaving the garden unattended facilitates the growth of weeds. The garden of spirituality will have its share of weeds in the form of:

- **Doubts:** When we pursue a spiritual path aligned with the larger purpose of life, there is a certain discipline that we practise methodically. However, when we look around, we may find people deviating from that path. There are times (again, due to the illusory energy of this world) when we tend to think 'Am I missing out on something?' The social media parlance is FOMO or the fear of missing out.

  To illustrate this example, the Gita recommends that we transcend the concept of vegetarianism to satvik prasadam. Freshly cooked vegetarian food transforms into prasadam when we lovingly and humbly offer it to Krishna Himself, for Him to taste our preparation, and we honour the remnants. Now, we may find people around us indulging in eating meat. This could lead to a momentary thought of FOMO.

- **Dilemma:** An extension of FOMO, discussed above, is dithering or wondering if we have made the right decision. Such fickle thoughts permeate the mind and make us waver. They question the very essence of why we have taken the noble and spiritual path. If we are spiritually weak, we get easily influenced by the temptations of the world. If we remain subservient to the mind, we can be eaten by the weeds of dilemma and go astray to waste this gifted human form of life.

- **Fear:** A hazardous weed that can grow is the questioning of the sustenance of spiritual practice, including questions on continuing on this path for life. The reason why it is to be treated as hazardous is because what stems as fear can take the shape of a convenient reason to not pursue a spiritual life any more. The fear accentuates doubts and dilemma further, causing us to lose hope in the process. There is a famous saying, 'When you feel like quitting, think about why you started'.

If we leave these weeds unattended, they become deep-rooted and pollute our personality massively. Central to nipping them at the bud stage is applying Vedic knowledge. It gives us the power to discriminate. Hence, knowledge is compared to a sword.

By acquiring Vedic knowledge, we overcome the weeds by:

- **Cutting through Doubts:** Given above is an example of a doubt that enters the mind and leads to FOMO. For us to cut through those weeds of doubt, we should invest our mind in a systematic study of the sastras (Vedic knowledge) under the tutelage of saintly people, combined with the spiritual practice of japa (mantra meditation). This three-pronged approach will thwart the entry of such polluted thoughts. At a macro level, there are many research studies on the harmful effects of meat-eating and its major impact on global warming.[1] At a micro level, no matter what the culinary experience is at the time of eating, the consciousness in which the animal would be at the time of its death is one of horror and that consciousness transfers into the meat that one consumes. It does disturb our consciousness and animalistic propensities like lust, anger and greed manifest in us over time. On the other hand, honouring prasadam is devoid of sin and, in fact, nourishes the body, mind and soul. It transforms us holistically: physically, mentally and spiritually.

- **Remaining Determined:** Remaining in the company of saintly people is in itself a source of Vedic knowledge. When we are in their midst, we don't indulge in gossip (prajalpa) but in learning and discussing subjects of a positive nature and ones that uplift our consciousness. This uplifted consciousness helps us stay on track and remain committed to spiritual principles.

- **Maintaining One's Steadiness in Their Spiritual Journey:** As the association with saintly people and the systematic study of Vedic scriptures becomes a way of life, it steers our mind in a certain direction. Notable among the scriptures are the Bhagavad Gita (spoken by Krishna)

---

[1] See https://www.theguardian.com/environment/2021/sep/13/meat-greenhouses-gases-food-production-study and https://www.ncbi.nlm.nih.gov/pmc/articles/PMC5620025/.

and the *Srimad Bhagavatam* (spoken about Krishna). These works are replete with inspiring stories about great personalities and the transforming events in their life. Disciplined study of the verses and their elaborate explanations have the potential to touch our heart deeply and raise latent yet fundamental questions in our mind.

TWENTY-FIVE

The Right Vision

Human Quality: Mindfulness

A wealthy merchant once had a severe headache. Despite trying various medication, the merchant continued to suffer in pain. The headache dragged out for more than a week. His friend recommended that he visit a mystic who was visiting the town the following day.

The well-to-do merchant approached the mystic at his ashram with sweets, fruits and gifts as an offering. He presented them at the mystic's lotus feet, paid obeisance and exchanged greetings.

'Son, how may I help you?' the mystic asked after greeting and enquiring about his well-being.

'Swamiji, I have a severe headache. It has been ongoing for more than a week now.'

'I see,' the mystic said.

'I have tried different medication, including home remedies, but to no avail.'

'I'll help you, son. Don't worry,' the mystic assured him, getting into a meditative state.

The mystic closed his eyes, meditated deep and, using his mystic powers, said, 'Son, make sure that from tomorrow onwards everything you see is green in colour. If you continue to see green persistently, your headache will be gone in three days' time.'

Thankful, the merchant bowed before him and left the ashram.

A week passed and the mystic was about to leave the town. Before leaving town, he decided to visit the rich merchant and enquire about his health. As the mystic made his way to the merchant's house, servants holding cans of green paint in their hands stopped the mystic.

Surprised, the amused mystic looked at the cans of green paint and asked, 'What is this?'

'We have been asked to paint everyone green if they want to enter this house,' said one of them, clad in green clothing. 'Our master only wishes to see the colour green.'

The mystic had one of his disciples explain to the servants who he was and called for the merchant. As soon as he heard that the mystic had come calling, the merchant rushed to the gate to welcome him.

As he entered the house, the mystic was bewildered to find that everything was green: green walls, green sofa, green chairs, green floor and even green clothes!

With a chuckle, the mystic asked the merchant, 'What is going on here?'

The rich man replied submissively, 'I'm just following your instructions to see only the colour green. So, I covered everything in green.'

Smiling, the mystic said, 'Instead of turning the world around you green, if only you had worn a set of green glasses. Then, everything would have looked green. You were trying to change the outside world, but you should have tried to change your world from the inside.'

In the Brahma Samhita (5.38), it is said,

premāñjana-cchurita-bhakti-vilocanena
santaḥ sadaiva hṛdayeṣu vilokayanti
yaṁ śyāmasundaram acintya-guṇa-svarūpaṁ
govindam ādi-puruṣaṁ tam ahaṁ bhajāmi

When one is endowed with the vision of love, one can see one's beloved everywhere. A devotee of the Lord has real love and affection for the Lord, and feelings and emotions for the Lord. Therefore, the devotee is able to see the presence of the Lord in every manifestation of this creation because his eyes are tinged with the ointment or the salve of love.

The verse above showcases the importance of having the right vision and how that shapes the way we live life. The right vision arises not from the eyes but from the ears. Let me explain. The first process in spiritual realization is sravanam (hearing): hearing from authorized speakers in disciplic succession. When we are connected to the right authority, we hear authorized knowledge and develop the right vision. Once we develop the right vision, we no longer focus on exteriors or attempt to bring about change in the world outside. Rather, we drive change from within. We strive for course correction from within and focus on self-improvement. It's famously said, 'Be the change you want to see in the world.'

Let's delve into the theme of self-improvement and discuss how that manifests in the way we behave, creating a positive aura around our personality and thereby positively impacting the people we interact with.

Those who dedicate themselves to self-improvement, demonstrate the following traits:

- **Harmony between Their Purpose, Passion and Profession:** People who commit to self-improvement, always introspect and look within for constant improvement and analyse how they can get more attuned to their purpose in life. Because they constantly look within, they are able to listen to the voice of their heart and what matters to them, both professionally and personally. They are able to bring in harmony between work and life. Bringing in this harmony is something Jeff Bezos, founder of Amazon, has been vocal about too in recent times. He opines: 'This work-life harmony thing is what I try to teach young employees and actually senior executives at Amazon too. I get asked about work-life balance all the time. And my view is, that's a debilitating phrase because it implies there's a strict trade-off.'[1] Instead of viewing work and life as a balancing act, Bezos believes that it's more productive to view them as two integrated parts. He adds, 'If I am happy at home, I come into the office with

---

[1] See https://www.businessinsider.in/tech/news/jeff-bezos-says-work-life-balance-is-a-debilitating-phrase-he-wants-amazon-workers-to-view-their-career-and-lives-as-a-circle-/articleshow/84093053.cms.

tremendous energy and if I am happy at work, I come home with tremendous energy.'[2]

With this harmony in place, we are able to do justice to the multiple roles that we play—that of a parent, working professional, friend and, of course, that of child to our parents.

- **Resilience in the Midst of Adversity:** When we constantly look within and focus assiduously on self-improvement, we focus on what change we can bring about. A key lesson from the Bhagavad Gita is: 'We have limited control over our circumstances, but we have unlimited control over our consciousness.' As an airplane takes off and we fly higher, the tallest of skyscrapers appear tiny. We don't have control over the size of the buildings, but we have control over how high we can go. Similarly, the apparent adversity that strikes is beyond our control, but we have unlimited control over the consciousness with which we respond. If we look within, elevate ourselves to a higher level of consciousness and become mentally tough, we build resilience to face challenging situations in life.

- **Integrity in Character:** As we double down on self-improvement, we seek to anchor our behaviour in line with the values that serve as our moral compass. We become more mindful in the way we think, in the manner we act and in our response to situations. As we become increasingly mindful and improve, we become more honest and truer to our conscience. Truth lays the

---

[2] See https://www.investopedia.com/news/bezos-says-worklife-balance-debilitating-phrase/.

pathway to integrity and instils the resolve to lead a life of character.

- **Dedication to Service Without Selfish Consideration:** As we look inward, we subconsciously direct our mind to focus on things only within our control. As a result, we no longer wait for the exteriors to change according to our whims and fancies. Rather, we strive to make a difference from within and seek to find ways to serve society to the best of our abilities. With primary focus on self-improvement and mindful behaviour, we never let loose to indulge in selfishness or a quest for sense gratification.

- **Self-confidence in Their Mission:** As we strive for self-improvement and see tangible positive change over time, we grow in confidence. More importantly, because of the focus exclusively on one's own behaviour, there is no undue comparison with others or advent of any sort of complex, both inferior and superior. The rigour to focus on the mission of self-improvement takes precedence.

- **Conservative in Choosing Their Intimate Associates:** 'Tell me who your friends are, and I will tell you who you are', goes a famous saying. The power of association is recognized and it matters deeply to people who are focused on self-improvement. The reason is simple: they wouldn't leave room for inadvertent external damage to a reputation built over time. As a result, they choose their associates carefully and prefer to associate with those who will help them push the bar higher.

TWENTY-SIX

Wonders of the World

Human Quality: Gratitude

A group of primary school students were on a day-long excursion. It was snack time, and biscuits and fruits were distributed on plates. The teachers made them sit in a circle in smaller groups. For the group activity, she gave each one of them a sheet of paper and a pencil.

In one such group, a teacher asked a question, 'Can you jot down the new wonders of the world?'

Munching on the biscuits, the children started to write their answers. All the children completed their list in two minutes. However, one student continued writing.

'One more minute left,' the teacher announced.

A minute passed and the student continued to write.

'Time's up, Smita,' the teacher notified. 'We need to finish here and move on to the next activity.'

The teacher went around the group. The students had put the following names on their list: the Taj Mahal, the Great Wall of China, the Pyramids in Giza, the Empire State Building, the Grand Canyon and the Panama Canal.

She praised all the students. It was Smita's turn next and the teacher noticed that she was still thinking and adding to her list.

Intrigued, the teacher called out, 'Smita, it's a straightforward question. I wonder why you need so much time to complete your answer?'

Smita replied, 'Yes ma'am. There are so many wonders. I'm still thinking.'

The teacher remarked, 'But I need only the top seven wonders.'

'That's ready, ma'am,' Smita replied with a smile.

'Please can you read them out,' the teacher said.

'To see, to touch, to taste . . .' Smita began, leaving the group wondering what this was about.

She concluded, beaming, 'To feel, to love, to laugh and to smell.'

Bewildered, the teacher looked at the girl and asked, 'Are these your seven wonders?' The rest of the students were confused too.

'Yes, ma'am,' Smita affirmed. 'Because even the simplest of experiences we have in our life are a matter of great wonder. If we take these for granted, we will not be able to appreciate their value and we won't be thankful to God. This is what my mother taught me.'

Therefore, the greatest wonder in the world is that we have everything available for us to experience satisfaction and joy. But still we keep searching for wonders outside of ourselves.

In the Bhagavad Gita (15.13–14), Lord Krishna says,

> *gām āviśya ca bhūtāni*
> *dhārayāmy aham ojasā*
> *puṣṇāmi cauṣadhīḥ sarvāḥ*
> *somo bhūtvā rasātmakaḥ*
> *aham vaiśvānaro bhūtvā*
> *prāṇinām deham āśritaḥ*
> *prāṇāpāna-samāyuktaḥ*
> *pacāmy annam catur-vidham*

I enter into the planet and keep it moving. I am the one who enters into the fruits and the vegetables and the plants, and gives them taste. I enter into the element fire and then create heat, which helps you cook the food, and I ultimately am there in the form of the fire of digestion, which helps you digest [your food].

This is an emphatic statement and unravels the source of the magic/mystery that we experience day in, day out. We get so used to enjoying the experience that we take it for granted. However, if we just take a pause, step back and look at the world with objectivity and without a tinge of any habituation, we become inquisitive to know more about such unfathomable phenomena. And as we submissively gather knowledge, our heart gets filled with humility and gratitude.

Smita unpretentiously presented the reflections of an unadulterated mind. The wonders—sense perceptions—described by the girl are just the tip of the iceberg. The Supreme Lord, Krishna, unconditionally presents us with such gifts in abundance, expecting nothing in return. Despite us wanting to live separate from Him, He creates a separate infrastructure in this material world. To facilitate our life in this world, He puts into a mechanism a divine medium called motherhood. Motherly love is divine and is considered the highest form of unconditional love in this world. Imagine a helpless newborn and the danger it faces in the absence of a mother! Such is the love that God has for us and the only means through which we aptly reciprocate is by expressing our gratitude.

Gratitude in Sanskrit is called krta + jna. 'Krt' means action and 'jna' means to remember.

Gratitude literally means remembering what someone has done for me. My spiritual master, H.H. Radhanath Swami, has spoken extensively on the topic of gratitude. I am happy to share excerpts from his teachings. The greatest loss in modern times has been a loss in the memory capacity of the people. The loss of memory finds its effects not just in forgetting names, numbers, data, etc., but it finds its most powerful impact in the forgetfulness of our best well-wishers with time.

Gratitude is a divine virtue that is so important that other divine virtues cannot exist without it. Spirituality grows like a seed within our heart. The goodness of our lifestyle protects that seed. Our spiritual practice of chanting God's names, reading scriptures, doing seva for God and others, waters that seed. But gratitude is what makes the ground fertile so that all these other virtues can actually have maximum effect. The fertile soil allows the seed to have deep roots and grow very strong, and, for that, a grateful heart is essential.

Gratitude is to see beyond the immediate circumstances that come upon us and to actually seek the essence of that situation, which is real wisdom. We need to see every situation as a beautiful opportunity to grow if we are to be grateful. All the dualities in life, success and failure, honour and dishonour, etc., are opportunities to learn something, to become better and grow. Ultimately, there is an opportunity in every situation to take shelter under the higher power of God. And in doing so, we find that life has inconceivable treasures in every moment. Therefore, to seek the essence, means to look for the hand of God in every situation. This is the spiritual definition of success.

If we simply lament when things go wrong, nothing will be accomplished. But if, in a difficult situation, we earnestly take shelter under the Lord and with our God-given ability attempt to fix and improve that situation, then we can reverse a curse into a blessing. The story of the greatest success in life often involves a person who hits rock bottom, only to discover something so beautiful and precious that if they didn't go through it they would have lived just a mediocre spiritual life and would not have accomplished much within.

Some people are ungrateful, no matter what. Even if you give them something wonderful, they want something more. That is why, while raising children, it's not good to spoil them. When children are accustomed to getting whatever they want and whenever they want, when they grow up, they are going to have the same conditioning. But the problem is that as an adult you do not get whatever you want and whenever you want. And then there is anxiety; sometimes that is very difficult to overcome.

Without gratitude, you cannot be satisfied in the heart. Because whatever you get, you feel you deserve and you want something more. And whatever you get, you feel it's expected or 'I should get this'. And when you don't get what you want, you complain and blame others saying, 'Why is the world against me?' Some people are never grateful.

And then there are those who are grateful when they get good things, but very much disturbed and bewildered when difficulties come into their lives. But the universal principle of all spiritual paths and a very basic principle of the Bhagavad Gita teaches that we should be grateful for whatever God gives us. For the good things that come, we should feel that 'I don't deserve this but I am so grateful!' Any bit of kindness that a person shows us, we should be grateful for it. Any blessings we receive, we should be grateful for it. And the difficulties, the pains, the failure, if we can be grateful for those, we could learn and grow through the experience. Otherwise, we miss a precious chance. We could learn to come closer to God, to improve the quality of our own lives and to overcome the obstacles that are holding us back. But those lessons that the Lord is always speaking from within our hearts can only be heard when there is gratitude.

TWENTY-SEVEN

The Creator[1]

Human Quality: Humility

Sir Isaac Newton had a friend who, like himself, was a scientist. Newton believed in God. However, his friend was an atheist. During many discussions, Newton would bring up the topic of God and attempt to make his friend understand how God was the creator of the marvellous universe that we live in. Each time, though, his friend would shake his head and refute him, saying that the universe 'just happened'.

After several such attempts, Newton decided to take one final shot at it to emphatically convey his point.

Newton had an accomplished artisan fashion for him a small-scale model of the solar system that was to be put in a room in Newton's home when it got completed. The assignment was finished and installed on a large table. The artisan had done a commendable job, simulating not only the various sizes of the planets and their relative proximities, but also in constructing the model in such a way that everything

---

[1] Adapted from 'The Sir Isaac Newton Solar System Story', *The Truth: God or Evolution?*, Marshall and Sandra Hall, Baker Book House, Grand Rapids, MI.

rotated and orbited when a crank was turned. It appeared as an interesting, even fascinating, work, particularly to anyone schooled in the sciences.

Newton invited his scientist friend home one day. That evening, after a brief chat, Newton took him around the house. In a while, they entered the room where the model had been erected. Casually, Newton showed him the room without paying attention to the marvellous model, which was the apple of his eyes, so to say.

'Oh my! What an exquisite thing this is!' Newton's friend exclaimed. 'Who made it?'

The friend was naturally intrigued on seeing the model and proceeded to examine it with undisguised admiration for the high quality of the workmanship.

Paying little attention to him, Newton answered, 'Nobody.'

Stopping his inspection, the visitor turned and said, 'Oh? Evidently you did not understand my question. I asked who made this?'

Newton, enjoying himself immensely, no doubt, replied in a still more serious tone, 'Nobody. What you see just happened to assume the form it now has.'

'You must think I am a fool!' the visitor retorted heatedly, 'Of course somebody made it. That person is a genius and I would like to know who that is.'

Newton then spoke to his friend in a polite yet firm way: 'My dear friend, this thing is but a puny imitation of a much grander system whose laws you know. And I am not able to convince you that this mere toy is without a designer and maker. Yet, you profess to believe that the great original from which the design is taken has come into being without either a designer or a maker! Now tell me by what sort of reasoning do you reach such an incongruous conclusion?'

The friend quickly understood how foolish he had been. He realized that there had to be a Master Designer and Creator for everything! He thanked Newton for helping him learn this fundamental fact of life.

In the Bhagavad Gita (10.8), Krishna says,

aham sarvasya prabhavo
mattaḥ sarvam pravartate
iti matvā bhajante mām
budhā bhāva-samanvitāḥ

In essence, it implies: 'I am the origin of everything and everyone in this creation, both in the material and spiritual world.'

In this verse, Krishna confirms the 'how' and the 'who' of creation.

Intelligent persons are able to see the hand of the Supreme Lord. When they dissect the details and the methods of creation, they become filled with wonder, respect, thankfulness and gratitude. When they worship Him with great joy in this mood, they, thus, make their lives successful.

Now, comes the question that is common among agnostics and atheists. How can one believe in a God that one cannot see?

We will address this using two principles.

- **Principle 1: Cause and Effect:** Rationalists will concur that there needs to be a cause for an effect. An event cannot happen at random and due to:
  o **Wind:** When there is a bulk movement of air, we experience that we call the wind. In the summer months, the wind is warm. In the winter months, it's chilly. We do not see the wind but we perceive the wind (the effect) and conclude that air (the cause) must exist. Without air, there is no wind. Likewise, without God, there is no creation.
  o **Puppet:** Another example is a puppet show. When we see puppets dance (the effect) beautifully in the story narrated, we deduce that there is a puppeteer (the cause) entertaining us from behind the curtain and running the show. It's foolish for the audience to think that the puppets are dancing on their own. It's equally foolish for the puppets to think that they are independent and that they are the source of entertainment. In fact, they are instruments of entertainment. Just like puppets, we are instruments of God, aided by a body with its five senses and the subtle elements (the mind, ego and intelligence).
  o **Arrow:** When we see an arrow in motion (the effect), we can infer that an archer (the cause) has shot it. Yes! People in archery classes can relate to this example. Else, we can jog our memory to our childhood days when we watched the Mahabharat and the Ramayana series on TV. If an arrow is in motion, the cause is an archer who has released it.

- o **Fan:** Imagine you've returned home from school/work on a hot summer day. The first thing that you'd do is to look for the switch to turn on the fan. That becomes our source of relief. Although we cannot see an electric current, we see the movement of the fan as the effect of electricity.
- **Principle 2: The Unseen is Proven by the Seen:** When we see pearls in a necklace, we can infer that there is a thread binding them:
  - o When we look at that beautiful necklace, we see the pearls but not the thread. That doesn't disprove the existence of the thread. In fact, the thread (the unseen) combines the pearls (the seen) to present a beautiful necklace. Likewise, the unseen God is the source of all the beauty that we see in His breathtaking and sometimes inexplicable creation.
  - o Let's discuss an object called the rose. When we think of that object, multiple thoughts emerge in our mind. Now, there are multiple ways in which we can bring it to life. We could pluck a rose from the garden. Or we could paint a rose on a sheet of paper. Or we could fold a paper to resemble a rose. But they are not the same and they present varied experiences. The rose plucked from the garden has four features: form, colour, fragrance and taste. However, the paper rose only has two features: colour and form. Lastly, the painted rose only has one feature: colour. In this way, we realize how the creations of God are full and complete, while our attempts to imitate them are reflections of the beauty but not complete.

In the Brahma Samhita, Lord Brahma offers prayers to Krishna, the Supreme Lord, after having emerged from the navel of Maha Vishnu. Therein, the first verse that Lord Brahma recites is:

īśvaraḥ paramaḥ kṛṣṇaḥ
sac-cid-ānanda-vigrahaḥ
anādir ādir govindaḥ
sarva-kāraṇa-kāraṇam

Krishna, who is known as Govinda, is the Supreme Godhead. He has an eternal, blissful spiritual body. He is the origin of all. He has no other origin and He is the prime cause of all causes.

To conclude, if we can accept and admire the finest painters, craftsmen and sculptors of all the wonderful creations by them, why not adore the supreme craftsman/sculptor, the source of it all—the Supreme Lord?

TWENTY-EIGHT

Holding on to Things

Human Quality: Mind Control

It was a moral science class for primary school students. Since it was a forenoon session and the students naturally fresh, the teacher wanted to present a thought-provoking concept. She brought a glass half filled with water.

As she held that glass in her hand, the teacher asked, 'Please tell me how heavy is this glass?'

One student quipped, 'Because it is half empty, it is not so heavy.'

Another one remarked, 'But it is half full, so it must be heavy.'

One more pointed out, 'It depends on how long you hold it.'

'Very well said,' the teacher praised them. 'Students, that's a very important point. If I hold on to it for a minute, well, it's not so difficult. It doesn't feel heavy. Rather, if I hold it for five minutes, it appears heavier and I begin to feel the pain.'

The students nodded in approval.

'But . . .' the teacher paused, looking around to draw the students' attention, 'if I hold it for an hour, it feels very heavy. More than that, it can be almost impossible to hold.'

She looked around the class to confirm if everyone was paying attention before she could present the lesson.

'Likewise . . .' she added, 'as we experience the world and interact with people, our minds are visited by bad thoughts like anger, greed, envy, jealousy, etc. Such bad thoughts fill the mind, similar to how water fills this glass. The longer we hold on to them, the heavier it feels.'

The students nodded in agreement.

In the Bhagavad Gita (6.7), Krishna says,

> *jitātmanaḥ praśāntasya*
> *paramātmā samāhitaḥ*
> *śītoṣṇa-sukha-duḥkheṣu*
> *tathā mānāpamānayoḥ*

When you conquer your mind and control your mind, that gives the ultimate experience of satisfaction and helps you rise beyond honour and dishonour, and fame and infamy. Then, you experience self-realization and God realization. Therefore, rather than thinking various kinds of thoughts, make sure you do not allow these thoughts to remain in your mind and bother you. And, therefore, you must replace these negative thoughts with positive thoughts by meditating on the messages coming in from divine sources and sound vibrations, which can be repeated in the form of mantras. These divine sound vibrations knock away these negative thoughts. Otherwise, carrying these negative thoughts is like holding a glass of water for twelve hours. The thought may be small, but because you're holding it in your mind for so long, it changes into worry and worry can really kill peace of mind.

Here are some basic guidelines that can help us keep the mind in control and remain free from anxiety:

- We should not be agitated and anxious when our plans fail due to providential impediments. More often than not, we formulate plans to accomplish a certain task with the hope that we succeed in it. However, if we become attached to the success element, that creates bondage. As a result of that bondage, when things don't go our way, we feel shattered and heartbroken. We tend to think that success is imperative if we just plan, strategize and put in the effort towards accomplishing it. However, there are multiple factors at play, which are beyond our control. To have peace of mind and composure, we should transform hope into prayer, with the understanding that the final outcome is dependent on the Supreme Lord. Thereby, we dovetail our efforts in the direction to please the Supreme Lord.

- We should always remember that when something happens due to providential arrangement, we should not feel sorry. As a follow up to what was discussed above, we need to take ownership of our efforts and dissect elements of how best we could have influenced the outcome. The final outcome is beyond our control and we definitely don't need to feel sorry about it. If something in our control was not best addressed, we should definitely repent for it and gather learnings from it. That said, lamenting over it is to be avoided.

- The more we try to rectify such reversals, the more we enter into the darkest regions of anxiety. Learning from the past and seeking to do course corrections for the future is welcome. However, constantly attempting to rectify reversals is a sign of living in denial. Research says that denial is the first stage in the change curve. As we continue to live in denial, it pushes us into darker regions of shock and anger. It's important that we deal with maturity, accept the past, learn from it and march ahead with gusto.

One great example of accepting reversals positively and leading a dharmic life were the Pāṇḍavas in the Mahabharata. The epic narrates in detail the unfairness meted out to them, the humiliation the siblings had to face and, not to mention, the attempted disrobing of Draupadi in the midst of the huge gathering. Despite this, the Pāṇḍavas endured such reversals successfully because they lived on higher principles and sought refuge there.

Let me throw light on the three guiding principles that made the Pāṇḍavas endure and emerge successful.

- **Guidance of the Sages:** The Pāṇḍavas deeply valued the sagacity of the learned souls. One such sage was Dhaumya, who practised severe penances at Utkocaka Tīrtha and was appointed royal priest of the Pāṇḍava kings. Dhaumya acted as the priest in many religious functions of the Pāṇḍavas (saṁskāra), and also each of the Pāṇḍavas was attended by him at their betrothal with Draupadi. Dhaumya was present even during the exile of the Pāṇḍavas and used to advise them in circumstances when they were perplexed. He instructed them how to live incognito for one year, and his instructions were strictly followed by the Pāṇḍavas during that time. In the Anuśāsana-parva of Mahabharata (127.15–16), Dhaumya gave religious instructions very elaborately to Mahārāja Yudhiṣṭhira. As the priest of the householders, Dhaumya guided them on the right path of religion.

- **Protection of Krishna:** Lord Krishna was everything to the unalloyed devotees, the Pāṇḍavas. He was for them the Supreme Lord, the spiritual master, a deity, the guide, the chariot driver, the friend, the servant, the messenger and everything they could conceive of. And thus, Krishna also reciprocated the feelings of the Pāṇḍavas. Simply by appreciating the dealings of the Lord with His pure devotees, one can attain salvation. The Pāṇḍavas were so malleable to the will of the Lord that they could sacrifice any amount of energy in the service of the Lord. And by such unalloyed determination, they could secure the Lord's mercy in any shape they desired. The Pāṇḍavas, by their unalloyed devotional service and full surrender unto the Lord, made it possible for the Lord to become a chariot driver or, at times, their messenger. Such duties executed by the Lord for His devotee are always very pleasing to the Lord because the Lord wants to render service to His unalloyed devotee, whose life has no other engagement than to serve the Lord with full love and devotion.

- **Their Own Actions Based on Dharma:** There are instances in the Mahabharata where the concepts of justice are boldly displayed, and no one would fault the Pāṇḍavas for taking action. At one point, the Pāṇḍavas and their mother are staying with a family in Ekachakra. Kunti finds out that the family is in dire difficulty. It's their turn to send off into the woods one family member as a sacrifice to a local rakshasa. Kunti is infuriated when she learns that it's too much of a botheration for the king of the land to protect the citizens of Ekachakra. She herself is a queen, but not the queen of their land. Nevertheless, she takes it upon herself to send her mighty son Bhima into the forest to correct this injustice. Another instance of injustice is the famous dice match, wherein Draupadi is dishonoured. The blind king, Dhritarashtra, appeals to Draupadi to excuse his sons for their offences against her. As a proper gesture, the king nullifies the dice game and returns to the Pāṇḍavas all the property they lost in the game. But the Pāṇḍavas vow to ultimately correct these wrongs and Arjuna is sent to the realm of the demigods to procure celestial weapons for the battle to come.

TWENTY-NINE

Maximizing Utility

Human Quality: Value

It was a chilly morning on the lush green campus of a college in Ooty. The winter had just set in and the students, clad in sweaters, were flocking to the campus. The classes began soon. It was the last day of one of the teachers on campus. The teacher spoke a few words of wisdom, shared her experience of teaching them and wished the students well. As a parting note, the students pleaded, 'Dear teacher, you have given us a lot of knowledge. We would like to offer you something in return.'

'That's so kind of you; thank you,' the teacher beamed. 'Well, if you do want to offer me something, then please find some useless, dry leaves and bring them to me.'

Though surprised, the students felt if that's what pleased the teacher, they would be happy to fulfil his desire.

The students went searching for dry leaves in the area surrounding the college campus. As they walked a few metres, they found some dry leaves. They were about to pick them up when, suddenly, a farmer came there.

The farmer shouted, 'Hello there. Don't touch these dry leaves.'

One student remarked, 'Why not? They are just lying here.'

'No,' he protested. 'I've kept them here for composting. Soon, they will turn into manure.'

'All right,' the students responded in wonder.

'Please do not take them. The manure is of great use to me.'

Obliging the farmer, the group of students made their way in search of dry leaves elsewhere. They reached another heap. They were just about to pick up those dry leaves when an old woman stopped them.

'Do not touch these dry leaves,' she warned. 'They will be used by me for making biodegradable plates.'

Again surprised, the students nodded.

'I'll just need to insert small sticks between them,' she added. 'And I will sell these plates in the market. They sell like hot cakes.'

'That's right,' one student remarked. 'People are becoming more environment conscious.'

Refused at yet another place, they moved on, hoping they would succeed in their next attempt. But, that was not to be. A middle-aged man stopped them now.

'Don't touch them,' he said. 'These leaves will be used in place of firewood.'

Used to this refusal game by now, the students moved on without exchanging a word.

Then, one of them quipped, 'We are unable to find dry leaves. Then let's get wet leaves. Let's pull them from water.' The group accepted the proposal and found a lake nearby.

As they reached the lake, they found one leaf floating on water. They went near the leaf, hoping no one would stop them this time.

As they were about to pick up that leaf, they saw an ant sitting on it. As they thought deeper, they realized that the leaf had actually become a lifesaver for that ant. They found that this leaf was useful too.

The students returned to the teacher and shared the lessons they had learned. That no leaf—dry or wet—was useless. People as well as even a tiny ant utilized them in their own ways.

In the *Srimad Bhagavatam* (11.2.29), it is said,

> *durlabho mānuṣo deho*
> *dehinām kṣaṇa-bhaṅguraḥ*
> *tatrāpi durlabham manye*
> *vaikuṇṭha-priya-darśanam*

This human form of life is rare. Rarer still is that person who understands the value of this human form of life and does not consider this human body to be useless and insignificant. He realizes this human form of life is very significant and must be utilized to ultimately attain the Supreme Lord by practicing the process of self-realization. One may not have money, one may not have assets, one may not have position but in spite of not having any of these significant material assets, one should not consider one's human form as useless. Instead, one should utilize it to remember the Supreme Lord and make one's life successful.

This verse explains the importance of the human form of life. This is important to realize because there are situations in life when people face multiple failures, sometimes in a succession. Now, what starts off as dejection can exacerbate into hopelessness, so much so that people question their very existence. Blinded by the shortcomings, they don't value what they have and feel their life is doomed. The story above illustrates how even a dry leaf has multiple purposes and that nothing in this world is useless. This human form of life is precious, and one needs to have the right understanding of the purpose of life to lead life with the divine vision.

The *Chanakya Niti* (7.20) lists four steps to rise in divinity. Purity is at the core of it all. Purity refers to a higher level of consciousness that the soul experiences.

- **Purity of Speech:** With purity in speech, one speaks politely, sensibly and sensitively. With purity in speech, one is able to avoid prajalpa, and unnecessary and foolish conversations. When one is pure in speech, one speaks the truth and doesn't indulge in manipulation.

- **Purity of Mind:** Purity of mind takes shape in the manifestation of thoughts. This is the root. As they say, 'Watch your thoughts, they become your words; watch your words, they become your actions; watch your actions, they become your habits'. Purity of mind also purifies the intent of action.

- **Purity of the Senses:** When the mind is pure, it acts as the central hub to spread purity to the senses as well. We see the right things, we hear the right things, we speak right and we also eat right. This implies that we are able to discriminate. We know what to take and what to leave. We are able to see the purity in others and as a result, we remain pure.

- **Purity of a Compassionate Heart:** Just as a pure mind leads to clean thoughts, a pure heart enables us to emote sensitively. A compassionate heart lets us understand people from their point of view and develop empathy. As a result, we become more selfless in our dealings and develop a willingness to serve.

The Divine compassion manifests in four ways in response to your focused dedication.

- Your willingness to serve brings empowerment and makes your service highly effective.
- Empowerment from the divine realm comes when you gladly offer all your expertise to help others.
- These divine connections will reciprocate by awarding you with increased responsibilities.
- As you provide excellent service by giving fully of yourselves, you will receive more complicated and difficult duties as a means of promoting and rewarding you because your dedication is appreciated.

THIRTY

Intelligence through Indirect Perception

Human Quality: Clear Thinking

It was a hot day along the coast. As he led his donkey carrying two sacks of wheat, Murari felt tired and sluggish due to the heat and humidity. Having travelled a good distance since the forenoon, Murari looked for a place to rest that afternoon. He spotted a tree and stopped there, tying the donkey to the tree. He unpacked his lunch box, ate some food and shared some with the donkey as well. Soon, he laid his mat under the tree to rest. Exhausted, he fell asleep right away. Almost two hours had passed when he woke up suddenly.

As soon as Murari got up, he noticed that his donkey was missing. Panicking, he jumped up and started looking in all the directions to see if the animal was grazing somewhere. He was worried since it was carrying two big sacks of wheat. He was supposed to sell the wheat to a merchant in town. Terrified, he frantically searched for the donkey. Then, he spotted a boy.

Murari asked him, 'Have you seen my donkey?'

'Well,' the boy thought for a moment. 'Is it the donkey that cannot see from its left eye?'

'Yes,' Murari replied, feeling hopeful.

'Is one of its foot injured and was it carrying wheat on its back?' the boy asked.

'Yes, of course,' the man was jubilant. 'Where did you see it?'

'Actually, I didn't see it,' the boy blurted. 'I just guessed it.'

Sensing something was amiss, Murari became angry.

'Come on,' he said to the boy. 'You described my donkey so accurately. How is it possible that you have not seen it?'

'No, sir,' the boy pleaded. 'Believe me. I haven't seen your donkey.'

'I'm sure you have it. You must have stolen that wheat,' Murari said, as he dragged the boy to a nearby police station.

The man informed a police officer in station, 'Officer, this boy says he has not seen my donkey but he described it accurately.'

'Noted,' the officer said. 'Boy, you seem honest. Please tell the truth. How could you describe the donkey accurately if you have not seen it?'

'Thank you for believing me, madam,' the boy replied. 'Let me explain myself.'

He continued, 'Madam, it is very simple. As I was walking along a stretch of road, I saw that grass only on the right side of the road was eaten. The grass on the left side was as it is. So I guessed that the animal that passed by must have been blind in the left eye. Then, I saw animal tracks on one side of the road but not on the other side. So I realized that the donkey must have been limping. My final observation was that there were grains of wheat strewn on both sides of the road. So, I realized that the donkey must have been carrying wheat on its back.'

Convinced by the boy's response, both the police officer and Murari praised him.

'And, madam,' the boy concluded, 'this town only has cows and dogs. I've not seen such animal tracks in a long time. So, I sensed that it must have been this man's donkey.'

One does not need to see everything to believe it. One can also understand based on symptoms and, therefore, it is described in the *Srimad Bhagavatam* (10.14.8),

> *tat te 'nukampām su-samīkṣamāṇo*
> *bhuñjāna evātma-kṛtam vipākam*
> *hṛd-vāg-vapurbhir vidadhan namas te*
> *jīveta yo mukti-pade sa dāya-bhāk*

When we go through distress and difficulties, we may not be able to see the main cause of our difficulty. But just like the intelligent boy in the story above, we can use our intelligence to surmise that we must have done something in our last life due to which we are getting the reaction in this life, for both good and bad. And therefore, if we simply tolerate this, then we become the rightful heir to the kingdom of God. Because what does a child have to do to gain the parent's property after the parent's passing? The child simply has to be a loyal child. And therefore, let us use our intelligence and understand that yes, the Lord has offered us the inheritance of the kingdom of God and eternal service at His lotus feet. We need to simply tolerate our difficulties and wait for the right opportunity when we can engage in that service eternally.

As they say, 'pain is compulsory, but suffering is optional.'

Hope is the lotus that springs out of the waters of authentic spiritual experience. The foundation for hope is the inner experience of joy stretched against the external experience of constant bombardment of miseries thrown at us.

The authentic spiritual experience is symptomized as being:

- **Mindful:** Being mindful is about being fully present, aware of where we are and what we are doing. At the same time, it is about not being overly reactive or overwhelmed by what's going on around us. Our state of mind is under control and we don't get swayed by external factors. Whenever one brings awareness to what one is directly experiencing via the senses or to the state of mind via thoughts and emotions, one is being mindful. Being mindful allows us to remain connected to the soul and in touch with our physical, mental, emotional and spiritual self.

- **Useful:** When we understand that our true position is being a part and parcel of God, we feel valued. More so, when the Supreme Lord has bestowed us with the human form of life, we realize that we are one step away from entering His eternal spiritual kingdom. Having reached such an important position, it's important we realize this. We must strive to be useful to society, add value and make a positive difference to those that we meet and interact with.

- **Faithful:** Being faithful reflects a heart filled with gratitude. When we are grateful to what has been bestowed on us, we remain keen to spread that positivity and be true in our relationships. When faithfulness blooms, we strive to do good and commit to selfless service for the welfare of others. We find pleasure in the happiness of others as we continue to contribute to that.

- **Joyful:** The nature of the soul, the spiritual spark/the real self, is saccitananda (full of knowledge and bliss). This spiritual bliss manifests in the joyfulness that one exhibits. This joyful behaviour helps one see the brighter side of life and cheers up even those who are dull. The optimism that flowers as a result makes them determined to pursue life with a razor-sharp focus on goals.

- **Merciful:** Being forgiving is a manifestation of a merciful heart. One who is merciful sees no ill will and possesses no ulterior motives. They possess high levels of tolerance and are not flustered by offhand comments here and there. They encourage people and explore ways to bring out the best in others.

THIRTY-ONE

The Value of Love

Human Quality: Love

There was an island on which all the feelings—Happiness, Sadness, Vanity, Richness, Knowledge and Love—lived.

One day, it was announced that the island was going to sink within hours. So, all of the feeling personifications got into boats and started to escape. Love, unfortunately, was not able to find a boat.

Suddenly, the water level started to rise, threatening Love with dire consequences. Love reached out for help everywhere.

Looking at Richness passing by in a boat, Love urged, 'Please take me in your boat.'

Richness responded, 'My boat is filled with the most valuable and precious jewels. Sorry, there is no space for you.'

Love called out to Vanity, who was passing by, and requested, 'Hey, please take me in your boat.'

Vanity snapped, 'My boat is spic and span. It looks so beautiful. Your presence here will make it messy.'

Dejected, Love called out to Sadness for help, 'Please. You can understand my difficulty. Please take me with you.'

Sadness said in a low voice, 'Well, I'm feeling so sad. I need to be alone. I need my space. So, I am sorry.'

At that point, Love was wondering who would lend it a helping hand. Out of the blue, one elderly person came in a boat. That elderly person picked up Love in the boat, sailed to the shores and transported Love to safety. Love met the rest of the feeling personifications there.

Panting, Love turned to Knowledge and asked, 'Who was this elderly person who saved me? Although I asked him, I did not get any response. Please tell me who brought this boat and rescued me?'

Knowledge said, 'Well, this person who rescued you is very special. It is Time personified.'

Amazed, Love sought further clarification, 'That was Time? But why did Time take the trouble to come and rescue me without me asking Time for help?'

Knowledge smiled and said, 'My dear Love, that is apparent. Only Time values contribution, only Time understands the real value of Love. No one else does. Give it Time and Love manifests in the hearts of people.'

There is a beautiful verse in the *Srimad Bhagavatam* (10.81.16),

> *kvāhaṁ daridraḥ pāpīyān*
> *kva kṛṣṇaḥ śrī-niketanaḥ*
> *brahma-bandhur iti smāhaṁ*
> *bāhubhyāṁ parirambhitaḥ*

When Sudama is made unlimitedly fortunate by Krishna, he offers his prayers of gratitude and says, 'The Supreme

Lord Krishna is unlimitedly merciful, that although He is the husband of the goddess of fortune, He decided to have a relationship with one who was devoid of fortune and made him filled with fortune.'

Therefore, we see here that the Supreme Lord is an emblem of love, an embodiment of supreme compassion. The Lord rewards the devotees through the agency of the time factor and punishes those who are sinful through the agency of the time factor. Hence, all we need to do is to simply serve and love the Lord with full energy and desire

Now, let's discuss the principles of love

- **Service without Selfish Considerations:** Service is a natural tendency in us as human beings. If we think about it, we serve different kinds of people at different stages and in different situations in life. Some of the day-to-day examples are serving parents by purchasing groceries, serving managers at the workplace, serving grandparents by fixing their mobile phones so they can watch videos of their choice, serving friends by sharing happiness, etc. Serving people is a natural way to give pleasure to the soul, our real self. However, due to false ego, we desist sometimes and, more often, we are not selfless. Conscious selfless service to one and all, not just human beings, but also to animals, birds and insects, is the starting point for love to blossom and, at the same time, this selfless service is an expression of love. In India, there is the tradition of drawing kolam using rice flour. It serves as food for tiny insects like ants, not visible to the naked eye. The same kolam also serves as an object of beauty for the visitor/guest.

- **Willingness to Experience Personal Pain to Give Pleasure to the Object of Our Love:** A farmer toils hard in the fields to sell grains and pulses in the market. He doesn't see this as a struggle but as an opportunity to serve his family's needs. This is visible on the day he returns home with gifts from the market. The family, on the other hand, view the challenges he undertakes by working under the sun and the austerity that he undertakes while maintaining the field as symbols of his love. This infuses gratitude in the hearts of his family members and they reciprocate that love in ways that they can express.

- **Investing in Spending Time to Grow Love:** A newly married couple invests a lot of time, as much in each other as much as possible, to express each other's feelings. They spend quality time to understand the other and be well-understood. Giving time to the partner amidst so many other activities that we do in a day is a symbol of love. We give time to make the partner understand how much they mean to us. Couples take time off from work to leverage long weekends to spend quality time together at wellness retreats or just spend time at home with extended family.

- **Listening to Feelings beyond Words, with Empathy, Knowing That We Are Not Self-sufficient:** In this world, we are not independent. We need each other to get through both the crests (happiness) and the troughs (sadness). In times of sadness, we need to listen to people with deep empathy and reveal our heart to be the pillar of support for them. Even in times of happiness, we need to share our joy with people. In fact, our happiness multiplies as we bond with people and share details of the celebration. As we seek to spend time getting the details of the celebration, people feel elated sharing details and we make them feel important too.

- **Have Deep Conversations Revealing One's Thoughts, Feelings and Fears to One Another without Inhibition and with Honesty:** Openness and transparency in conversations is very important to build long-term relationships built on the foundation of love. Obscurity and ulterior motives have no place and one should be candid in expressing one's feelings. Even if one is expressing doubts or fears, one should be polite in sharing them with objectivity (with examples preferably) and speak one's mind. As long as we remain true to conscience and show the right intent, people will not misunderstand us. Rather, they will be understanding. Even if they were to misunderstand us, we need to have deeper conversations to make the other person understand us better. Showing affection and having deep conversations remain the best means to mend fences.

THIRTY-TWO

Calm before the Storm

Human Quality: Preparedness

There is a story about a sea captain who, in his retirement, skippered a boat taking day trippers to an island. On one trip, the boat was full of young people.

The voyage was about to begin. As was the norm, the devout captain prayed to the Almighty for two minutes.

Looking at the captain, the youngsters seated near him laughed at him.

One of them remarked, 'Who prays these days!'

The captain smiled but kept quiet.

Another remarked, 'Even then, when the day is fine and the sea calm, what is the need to pray, I wonder.'

Unprovoked, the captain went about his business. As they sailed deep into the sea, it wasn't long before they were hit by a storm. The boat began to roll and pitch violently. This was not expected as the weather forecast had said it would be a sunny day with clear skies.

The passengers, all youngsters, were terrified and horrified by what they imagined as the eventuality in such awkward weather conditions. Each one of them started to pray. Some of the prayers were so loud that they could be heard even amidst the thunderous waves.

The captain was unmoved and was at work. Those seated near the captain yelled at him and pleaded with him to join them in their prayers.

Calmness personified, he replied, 'I say my prayers when it's calm. When it's rough, I attend to my ship.'

If we cannot seek God in the quiet moments of our lives, we are not likely to find Him when trouble strikes. We are more likely to panic. But if we have learnt to seek Him and trust Him in quiet moments, then, most certainly, we will find Him when the going gets rough.

In the Bhagavad Gita (2.41), Krishna says,

> *vyavasāyātmikā buddhir*
> *ekeha kuru-nandana*
> *bahu-śākhā hy anantāś ca*
> *buddhayo 'vyavasāyinām*

This verse implies that we must pursue the spiritual path with business-like professionalism and focus. Knowing that if we invest every single day carefully and with the proper kind of consciousness, realizing the value of every moment, we will be able to remember the Lord properly when the storm of death comes. That is the true profit in the human form of life. Before going to bed every day, it's a good practice to prepare our balance sheet of how many moments we forgot about the Lord and how many moments we actually remembered the Lord. If the remembrance is more than forgetfulness, then the balance sheet is profitable.

Further, this verse describes how we need to pursue it with professionalism and focus. Let's shift focus to prescribed duties. In the story above, when the storm struck, the captain conducted his prescribed duty with professionalism. For some, it remains an act of wonder as he rightfully performed his prescribed duties without compromising on his spiritual consciousness.

The Bhagavad Gita (18.7–9) throws light on this theme. It describes prescribed duties and classifies them at three levels:

- If prescribed duties are renounced because of illusions, such a renunciation is said to be in the mode of ignorance. If the captain had been lazy when it came to performing his duty, reluctant to pilot the ship at that time or in a state of depression as a result of the situation that he was in, he would have been said to be in the mode of ignorance. Often times, people who travel in the sea are intoxicated to avoid the real experience that comes along with the journey. That gives them the illusion that they are in a different realm altogether and in such an inebriated state, one is again said to be in the mode of ignorance.

- If prescribed duties are given up because they are troublesome or out of fear of bodily discomfort, such a renunciation is in the mode of passion. If the captain had abstained from performing his duty and panicked due to the storm, just like the others in the boat, then he would have been said to be in the mode of passion, gripped by fear of bodily discomfort. Fear grips a person and makes him fearful of his life when he ties that fear to his body.

The real understanding is that we are not the body but the spiritual soul, as Krishna confirms.

- If one performs his prescribed duty in the following ways, then such renunciation is in the mode of goodness:
  - o **Only Because it Ought to Be Done:** In the story above, the captain had a unique role to pilot the ship. Multiple people boarded the ship with the faith that they were in safe hands. Hence, the onus is on the captain and he ought to have performed this duty righteously.
  - o **Renounces All Material Associations:** In the story above, we had a peek into the sense of calmness with which the captain responded to the tough situation that he was in. It was visible that neither was he afraid of the attack nor did he look for material relatives/ association among passengers in the ship for him to act dutifully. He performed a selfless act of service by best displaying his skills.
  - o **Gives Up All Attachment to the Fruit:** In here, it was clear that the captain exhibited a positive demeanour and gave hope to the passengers in the form of his calmness. However, he explicitly mouthed no words of the rescue operation being successful. He operated with the right understanding of a dutiful captain steering the ship to the best of his abilities. He had the correct understanding that the outcome of the rescue rested in the hands of God.

The conclusion is that we need to perform our duties:

- without any doubt
- without attachment to auspicious work
- without hatred of inauspicious work

THIRTY-THREE

The Cursed Kingship

Human Quality: Preparedness

There was a royal kingdom that followed a rather unique style of functioning. The kingdom in itself was heavenly, consisting of the richest of treasures, pure water, first-class vegetation, highly respectable ministers, hardworking labourers and mighty armed forces. However, there was a rule that kingship was awarded for a year only. At the end of the year, the king would be sent to a nearby island, which was inhabited by ferocious wild animals, terrorizing birds and scary insects. Further, the island was impoverished as well.

The kings enjoyed ruling for a year but ended their tenure on a wretched note, as they were forced to spend the remainder of their lives on a distant island with limitations and threatening consequences. While most kings understood the implications and complied with life after kingship, some refused to and were dragged to the island by their ministers. Sometimes, the citizens too joined the procession.

In such circumstances, a new king would arrive. He would take charge, well-informed of the might of his armed forces, the loyalty of the ministers and the hardworking labour class. The populace in general showed great reverence to the king during his tenure and remained submissive. That was the reason why leaders were attracted to kingship despite the demoralizing consequences.

As soon as the new king took charge, he asked his ministers, 'At the end of this one year, I'll be sent to the island, won't I?'

They said, 'Yes, your highness.'

'But,' the king continued, 'for this one year, I am your king and you will obey my orders.'

'Absolutely, your highness. Your wish is our command.'

Eleven months passed by. History showed that kings exhibited signs of depression and a state of despair in their final month. Some of them lived in denial, while others lost their mental balance in anticipation of what was in the offing. However, this king was different. The citizens were surprised to see the king travel around the kingdom as majestically as he had done at the beginning of his rein, fully in charge of the affairs of the kingdom, a self-assured personality with no change in his behaviour from day one. His personality roared like a ferocious lion. The populace awaited the last day of his kingship.

At last, the farewell day arrived. Right at dawn, as had been the norm, thousands of people thronged the palace awaiting the scenes that were going to unravel in front of them. Specifically, the track record of this king, who remained calm even in the concluding month, was a shift from normal. A sense of excitement reverberated in the air.

The king made his way to the large courtyard, where the transfer of ownership happened and the sequential procession of the king to the island began. Unlike scenes that marked the painful exits of his predecessors, the king handed over the throne to his successor with a smile and made his way out. Just as he was exiting the palace to get into the cart waiting to drop him to the island, a middle-aged man walked up to the king and stopped him.

'My dear king, may I ask you a question?' the man asked politely.

'Yes, sir. Please.'

'Are you aware of what awaits you next?' the man mumbled. 'Do you know what danger awaits you on the godforsaken island?'

'Oh! Yes, I am aware of what awaits me next,' the king smiled, oozing confidence.

This response shook the populace. Never before had they seen a king keep his chin up.

Taken aback by the assurance, the middle-aged man added, 'But, in the past, we have seen kings respond very differently at the end of their tenure. Some of them left dejected, some turned mentally ill, some even had to be dragged away while they begged for relief. Now, I see you behaving very differently as you make your way out majestically, as though you are looking forward to taking up the next throne.'

'Yes,' the departing king roared. 'That's right. I am certainly taking the next throne.'

The man was speechless. 'But . . .' he murmured.

The king went on stage and addressed the audience: 'I understand that you all must be surprised like this gentleman based on what you have witnessed with the previous kings. But I am different. Let me explain.'

There was pin-drop silence as the king paused. Each and every person in the courtyard listened to the king with rapt attention.

'The last one year has been my kingship. I was the king, and each and every person here had to obey my orders. I was blessed with loyal and intelligent ministers, mighty armed forces and hard-working labourers. Awaiting what was to come to me at the end of one year, I ordered them to organize a boat. I landed there. I took with me a hundred strong men, both physically and mentally. Along with them, a few ministers, who are my confidants, and hard-working labourers.'

That was an eye-opener for the people. The ministers were flummoxed as they had no hint of what their superior was up to. They waited to hear more.

'As soon as we reached the island, with the armed forces, we put up tents and shot dead the ferocious animals and birds. We revamped the vegetation of that region. We found the bodies of the previous kings, which lay as is there. Now, the topography of the island has been overhauled with variegated flora and fauna. We leveraged the facility of this kingdom and the riches to construct my palace there, and to make cottages for ministers and settlements for the labourers. It's another beautiful kingdom that I have set up there.'

The people were amazed by the proactiveness, courage and clever attitude of the king. The ministers and the armed forces were in admiration of such a shrewd personality.

The king concluded, 'While I kept travelling between the two places, those men are stationed there even now. I couldn't enjoy the present kingdom as near-death awaited me but kept preparing for my future.'

There was a thunderous applause from the audience.

As per the tradition and custom, the king was made to sit on an elephant. The citizens paraded the beaming king across the city. He made his way to the island joyfully.

This story is a lesson on the importance of long-term planning, preparation and execution. The precursor to these is understanding ground realities. The king took up the role, well aware of the ground realities. But unlike his predecessors, he had a roadmap in his mind and executed it assiduously without any ruckus.

The inspiration that we need to draw from the king is how to plan our kingship called life, well aware of the ground realities of the four miseries of life: birth, old age, disease and death. No matter who we are, our kingship of life has its conclusion in death, similar to the condition the king above was to be subjected to. However, unlike his predecessors, he didn't fall into that trap but circumvented it due to his intellect, planning and assiduous execution.

In the Padma Purana, there is a verse,

smartavyaḥ satataṁ viṣṇur
vismartavyo na jātucit
sarve vidhi-niṣedhāḥ syur
etayor eva kiṅkarāḥ

The goal of life is to remember Lord Krishna at every moment. Life is a preparation; death is an examination. We should prepare our life in such a positive way by remembrance of the Lord, that at the time of death remembrance automatically happens and we're able to enter into the eternal abode of the Supreme Lord.

There is a similar verse in the Bhagavad Gita (8.5). An excerpt from it is says,

anta-kāle ca mām eva
smaran muktvā kalevaram

Here, Krishna says that if you think of me at the time of death, you come back to me without fail. This is the promise that someone no bigger than Krishna makes. This is not an ordinary assurance. Just as we say 'as sure as death', as sure as this promise.

Before we delve into how to prepare for this final examination called death, which strikes at a certain point in time, let's take a step back and take a macro look at the material world that we live in and the larger timelines that we are operating within.

There are four yugas—satya, treta, dvapar and kali—that make up one divya yuga of 4,320,000 years. One thousand such yugas make one day of Brahma, whose lifespan is a hundred years. Now, we get a sense of the timeline scale being shifted to billions of years.

Each yuga is an age with specific characteristics, in which incarnations of Krishna appear. In each yuga there is a specific process of self-realization (yuga dharma). The satya yuga (also called krta yuga when Lord Matsya appeared) is the golden age and lasts 17,28,000 years. The process of self-realization in this yuga is meditation on Vishnu. During this yuga, the majority of the population is situated in the mode of goodness and the average lifespan at the beginning of the yuga is 1,00,000 years. The treta yuga (when Lord Rama appeared), also called the silver age, lasts 12,96,000 years and the process of self-realization is the performance of opulent yajnas (sacrifices). The average lifespan is 1,00,00 years and the godly qualities decrease one-fourth compared with the satya yuga. The dvapar yuga (when Lord Krishna appeared) or the bronze age lasts 8,64,000 years and the process of self-realization is the worship of deities within temples. Godly qualities are reduced to 50 per cent as compared to satya yuga and the average life expectancy is only a thousand years. The current times that we live in is called kali yuga (when Lord Chaitanya Mahaprabhu appeared) or the iron age of hypocrisy and quarrels, and lasts 4,32,000 years. Lord Krishna appeared in His original, transcendental form and departed right before the beginning of kali yuga. The process of self-realization in this yuga is sankirtana, the chanting of the Holy Names of the Lord. God consciousness is reduced to 25 per cent of the population and life expectancy is only a hundred years. As on date, more than five thousand years of kali yuga have passed.

Now, in kali yuga, with the maximum duration of life being just a hundred years and that combined with various difficulties, the recommended process of self-realization is that of hearing and chanting of the holy name of the Lord. The holy name of the Lord is the Hare Krishna maha mantra: Hare Krishna Hare Krishna Krishna Krishna Hare Hare Hare Rama Hare Rama Rama Rama Hare Hare.

The *Chaitanya Charitamrita* (Madhya Lila 6.242) states,

harer nāma harer nāma
harer nāmaiva kevalam
kalau nāsty eva nāsty eva
nāsty eva gatir anyathā

In this age of quarrel and hypocrisy, the only means of deliverance is the chanting of the holy names of the Lord. There is no other way. There is no other way. There is no other way.

Now, let me summarize the various aspects of the powerful Holy Name (the Hare Krishna maha mantra) as we leverage this to suitably prepare ourselves for the final examination called death.

The Holy Name is the most powerful means of purification and atonement because:

- it has the highest power to purify
- it awakens devotion
- it is effective in all moods
- it is effective in all circumstances
- it counteracts all sins
- it acts even on those who are ignorant about its power

THIRTY-FOUR

The Priceless Diamond

Human Quality: Value

On the shores of the ocean, a fisherman caught a giant fish. A prized catch, as they say!

Curious, he looked intently at the fish's body parts. When he opened the stomach of the fish, he was amazed to find a diamond. Taken aback initially, he wondered what to do with it. He took a few minutes to come to terms with the fact that he actually possessed a diamond.

After thinking it through, he took the diamond to a merchant in exchange for money.

Gazing at the colossal diamond, the merchant was keen to seize it. At the same time, he was certain that the fisherman hadn't fathomed the magnitude of his possession. As a seasoned merchant, applying the tricks of the trade, he said, 'I can give you a whopping thousand gold coins for it.'

The thought of a thousand gold coins overwhelmed the fisherman. He thought to himself, 'That's my annual earning. Let me get rid of this before he lowers the value.'

As expected by the merchant, the fisherman accepted his offer right away. The diamond was sold to the merchant.

Money-minded that he was, the merchant took the diamond and brought it to the notice of the king. In a bid to gain the upper hand, he elaborated on the richness of the diamond, its rarity and the inherent value associated with it.

The king took one deep look at the diamond and was astonished. He had never seen a diamond so lustrous. It radiated a magnetic effect around the area.

Right away, the king asked the merchant, 'What's your price?'

The merchant said, 'Dear king, a million gold coins.'

The king immediately handed over one million gold coins and took possession of the diamond. Ecstatic and proud, the merchant left the palace

In a few minutes, a sage entered the king's palace. Seeing him, the king bowed down and welcomed him. They exchanged greetings and spoke briefly. A while later, the king showed the sage the diamond.

The learned sage took one look at the diamond and remarked, 'I hope you're not planning to sell this diamond.'

Keen to know more, the king said, 'Well, I just acquired it for one million gold coins.'

The sage added, 'Respected king, this kind of diamond is no longer available. It's the rarest of rare commodities; a possession of yore, I must say.'

'I see,' the king sighed.

'Yes, should you sell this diamond, it will be the greatest disaster,' the sage advised. 'It's truly priceless.'

The king was happy to receive this timely advice from the sage and gathered more information on the historical and scriptural details of the times when such a diamond was used.

In some time, the sage left the palace. The king bowed down and sought his blessings. Then, he carefully put the diamond in the treasury and would offer it to special guests to adorn them whenever they visited or on special occasions. This was a means for the king to show his affection and to make them feel special.

If all our desires in life are like an ocean, the human body is like a boat endowed with the power to cross over. This ocean of desires is guided by the guru (the captain), the sails of holy scriptures and the winds of favourable circumstances. The wisdom of the wise helps us become better sailors to navigate the ship well during periods of unexpected and prolonged storms in life.

There are various classes of transcendentalists. There are those who believe in fruitive work. They want something in exchange for their work, just like the fisherman wanted something in exchange for the diamond and so did the merchant. So, the karmis and the jnanis are the ones who need something in exchange for their effort. The karmis look for enjoyment and the jnanis look for liberation. But the devotee is represented by the king, who is advised by the great sage not to give up this diamond in exchange for anything.

In the Siksāstakam verse 4, Lord Chaitanya Mahaprabhu calls out,

na dhanaṁ na janaṁ na sundarīṁ
kavitāṁ vā jagad-īśa kāmaye
mama janmani janmanīśvare
bhavatād bhaktir ahaitukī tvayi

Lord Chaitanya Mahaprabhu prays, 'I do not want anything in exchange for devotional service. The devotional service itself is like a priceless diamond. And therefore, I do not want wealth, I do not want followers, I do not want fame, I do not want any kind of beautiful women in return for practicing devotional service. All I want is causeless devotional service at your Lotus Feet birth after birth. My dear Lord, please bless me with this kind of ahaituki bhakti.'

THIRTY-FIVE

The Foolish King

Human Quality: Wisdom

Once upon a time, a guru and his disciple were travelling from country to country. They stopped in a kingdom where they were astonished to find that everything sold at a flat rate of one gold coin per kilo. Be it silver, rice, vegetables, sweets, cereals, metal, etc.

Realizing this, the disciple was ecstatic and said, 'I want to settle down in this kingdom, guru ji, please allow me to do so.'

Surprised, the guru shot back, 'Why would you do that?'

'Because it's such a fantastic kingdom. Everything is about one gold coin per kilo. I love sweets and I can feast on them when they are available at such a low price.'

'Don't be foolish,' the guru emphasized. 'This king has no sense of value and does not know how to discriminate. Such a person can be very dangerous and foolish too.'

'Let us stay here for a few days, please,' the disciple urged.

'There's no way I'm going to stay here.'

'At least let me stay here for a month while you return to this country after visiting the nearby regions.'

'I do not recommend staying here,' the guru advised. 'You may land in trouble.'

Following the disciple's earnest appeals, the guru obliged him and moved on to the nearby country.

The disciple took charity from the people in the kingdom. As per his wishes, he was able to purchase ample quantity of sweets. Being physically away from the guidance of his guru, he became lax, gobbled sweets and whiled away his time eating and sleeping for days. As weeks passed, he realized that he had gained weight. Still, the need to gratify himself with additional sweets remained. He splurged on them unabashedly.

In a village in that kingdom was a villager who owned three goats. One day, one of his goats jumped on the neighbour's compound wall. Suddenly, that wall collapsed. As a result, the goat fell and died. That angered the villager. He told the neighbour to compensate him for the dead goat but to no avail. He explained his predicament, but the neighbour didn't budge and shifted the blame on others.

Finally, the villager approached the king in the palace, 'My dear king, there is injustice happening in your kingdom.'

Surprised, the king asked, 'What happened?'

'Well, my goat was standing on the neighbour's wall, and the neighbour's wall collapsed and my goat died.'

Not thinking even for a moment, the king said, 'I order that we hang the wall.'

Puzzled, the villager questioned, 'How does one hang the wall, O king? The wall is an inanimate object. You should hang the neighbour.'

'That's right,' the king said. 'I order that we hang the neighbour. Call him.'

The neighbour was brought to the king's court.

'It was your wall,' the king said. 'The goat died as a result of the poorly constructed wall. So, we will hang you.'

Taken aback, the neighbour said, 'But it was a mason who built the wall. Hang him.'

'That's right,' the king nodded. 'Okay, call the mason. We will hang him.'

The neighbour directed the courtiers to call for the mason.

When the king communicated the decision, the mason was dumbfounded. 'O king! Actually, my tailor poked one of my eyes with a needle. Because of that, I could only see with one eye. Thus, this wall ended up being poorly constructed.'

'I see,' the king said.

'So, please hang the tailor,' the mason requested.

When the tailor arrived, the king questioned, 'Why did you poke his eyes with your needle? We will hang you.'

Crying in self-pity, the tailor submitted his story, 'Respected king, it wasn't me. It was the needle that poked his eyes. That needle was made by a blacksmith. You should hang him instead.'

Not realizing the game of musical chairs at play here, the foolish king called for the blacksmith.

The blacksmith, a submissive worker, was bewildered at hearing the king's words that he would be hanged. Totally unaware of the sequence of events that had preceded his entry in the king's court, he remained silent.

The king pronounced that in fifteen days he would be hanged. Horrified, the blacksmith turned pale and hardly ate anything in the ensuing two weeks. He became too weak to even move. Having lost a lot of weight, he became thin. As lean as a pencil, as they say!

On the day of his hanging, he was taken in a procession to the scaffold. Unable to walk, he was dragged to the top of the frame. The king was seated right opposite the scaffold and witnessed the event along with fellow villagers. Incidentally, the disciple's guru also arrived in the village. Seeing all the villagers gathered together, he joined the scene as well.

The guards tried to put the noose around the blacksmith's neck but the noose was so loose that it would not fit.

The king's minister said, 'The noose is too loose, O king. Therefore, it does not fit his neck.'

'How can that be?' the king yelled.

'Sorry, but . . .' the minister explained the situation.

'All villagers are gathered here,' the king told himself. 'If we don't hang someone here, it will be a matter of huge shame for me. I'll have to hang someone here.'

The king then announced, 'Minister, find someone else. Find somebody who is fatter and whose neck will fit the noose.'

The minister was confused and wondered how that was fair.

'But, king, how can I . . .' the minister tried to reason with the king.

'Do as I say,' the king shot back. 'I am the king and you must follow my orders.'

In desperation, the minister went around the crowd and spotted the disciple. He looked stout and in the minister's assessment, his neck would fit the noose.

As the disciple was called, he was terrified. He asked, 'What wrong have I committed?'

The minister retorted, 'Your neck fits the noose and so you are the right man.'

'But, how is that a valid reason?' the disciple yelled, shaking in fear.

'No arguments,' the king announced. 'Hang him!'

The disciple recalled his guru's words on how the king must be someone who was unable to discriminate.

Respectfully remembering him, the disciple cried out, 'Oh, my dear guru, where are you? What you said is absolutely right.'

Standing in the corner of the crowd, the guru saw his disciple about to be hanged. Seeing his pitiable state, he walked up to the scene. Seeing a saintly person, the king stood up and bowed before him.

'Can I help make this boy understand the situation?' the guru asked the king.

'Yes, please do,' the king nodded.

The guru walked up to the disciple and whispered something into his ears.

Then, he walked up to the king and pleaded, 'My dear king, please do not hang him. Hang me, I am his guru.'

Surprised at the turn of events, the king said, 'But, why do you want to be hanged?'

'O King, it's my request that you hang me.'

The villagers were confused by what was happening there. Right from the neighbour and the mason to the tailor, who were all present at the site, everyone was dumbstruck at the scene unfolding before their eyes. Although weak, the blacksmith turned curious about what was going to happen and looked up.

'Why do you want to be hanged now?' the king thundered. 'I don't understand.'

'Now is the perfect moment to die,' the guru elaborated. 'Whoever dies at this moment, at this muhurta, he shall become the emperor of the world in the next life. Therefore, please give me this benediction.'

The king rose from the seat and said, 'What are you saying? It's such an auspicious moment and nobody here told me about it. I will not allow you or your disciple to die.'

The disciple felt relieved while the guru watched the king intently.

'I want to be hanged,' the king announced. 'So that I die at this opportune moment to become the emperor of the world in my next life.'

Unable to bear the antics of the king, the minister executed the order right away.

Gratitude in full display, the disciple prostrated before the guru and thanked him for saving his life. He regretted his mistake and assured him that he would always follow his instructions in life.

The Bhagavad Gita (4.39) presents a beautiful verse in this regard,

> *śraddhāvāḷ labhate jñānaṁ*
> *tat-paraḥ saṁyatendriyaḥ*
> *jñānaṁ labdhvā parāṁ śāntim*
> *acireṇādhigacchati*

One who is foolish, doubtful and one who does not have the right discrimination will ultimately perish. Therefore, human life is meant for utilizing one's intelligence so that we can discriminate between right from wrong, appropriate from inappropriate and make the right choices.

Further, as per Vidura Niti (chapter 1, text 31), here are ten symptoms of a fool with an uncontrolled mind:

- **Busy with Other's Activities:** Foolish people poke their noses into the affairs of other people. Instead of looking inward and striving to improve the self, they derive pleasure in finding faults in others. As a result, they continuously monitor the behaviour and actions of others superficially with the intent of fault finding.
- **Lacks Discrimination in Desires:** A foolish person is also called godās ('go' meaning mind and 'dās' meaning servant). Godās is a servant of the mind. They follow all that the mind asks for and have no power to control the mind. A goswāmi (master of the senses) is one who controls the mind and has the power to regulate the desires of the mind.
- **Envies the Powerful:** A foolish person has an inferiority complex that he/she is full of envy. If they were to meet someone better/more powerful, envy permeates their heart as they notice some of those qualities lacking in them. They don't get naturally inspired by their higher qualities nor do they learn from them.
- **Misunderstands a Friend to Be a Foe and a Foe to Be a Friend:** A foolish person lacks the power to differentiate between people. They are not observant and are ignorant about looking deep within people. They get cheated by superficial propensities that they see in people and draw naïve conclusions about them.

- **In Actions, They Doubt Everything and Spend a Long Time in Doing That Which Can Be Done Quickly:** A foolish person is pessimistic and doubts everything. They are not rational or logical people who reason out things and accept them once convinced. They keep finding faults with an intent of one-upmanship. Because they are doubters and indulge in finding faults, they are unable to identify themselves with a coherent thought process and commit to performing actions in a certain way. They remain indecisive and take longer to complete tasks.

- **Enters a Place Uninvited:** A foolish person lacks decorum in behaviour and acts on the mind's whims and fancies. For example, say, if they come to know of a friend attending a large gathering to meet people of repute and dine together, out of greed and uncontrolled desire, they will just walk into the place uninvited. With them, there is not even a question of expressing desire and taking permission to attend. They are always discourteous.

- **Speaks Much without Being Asked:** Foolish people give unsolicited advice. Due to their inferiority complex, they always seek to project themselves as people who are superior or worthy of admiration. They speak more than they listen.

- **Rationalizes His Own Mistake and Blames Others:** Besides finding fault (as discussed above), they also have the avoidable quality of not accepting their own mistakes despite realizing them. One who doesn't realize it acts in the mode of ignorance, while one who rationalizes even after realizing operates in the mode of passion and lives in denial.

- **Though Weak yet Has Powerful Anger:** They lack the power of knowledge and intelligence; yet due to a sense of entitlement, intolerance and impatience, they express it in the form of anger. They think that they can control people and express their authority by showing their anger. That gives them a sense of superiority complex.
- **Aspires Beyond Abilities with Inadequate Means:** Foolish people are unaware of their true capabilities. They live in denial and assume a higher sense of accomplishment and capacity. As a result, they aim for the sky when they are not even worthy of the treetop.

THIRTY-SIX

The Lord Listens to Our Sincerity

Human Quality: Divinity

Dr Mark, a well-known cancer specialist, was once on his way to an important conference in another city. He was going to be recognized with a global award for his path-breaking contributions in the field of medical research. He was excited to attend the conference as this recognition was a result of his hard work over decades. He believed that this was well-earned and that he deserved the award. As planned, he boarded the flight for the conference.

Two hours after the plane had taken off, it made an emergency landing due to a technical snag at the nearest airport. Worried that he wouldn't make it in time for the conference, Dr Mark immediately went to the reception. He frantically enquired about the next flight to his intended destination. Disappointed to learn that it would take off after ten hours, he looked for alternate aways to travel to the conference. The receptionist suggested that he rent a car and drive himself down to the city, which was only five hours away.

Despite his hatred of driving long distances on his own, he agreed to the idea. Dr Mark rented a car and began the journey. However, soon after he left, the weather conditions became overcast and a heavy storm surrounded the region. The heavy downpour made it very difficult for him to drive. Unfortunately, he missed a turn and took the incorrect road.

After an hour of driving, he realized that he had lost the way. Driving in heavy rain on a deserted road, feeling hungry and tired, he desperately looked for a sign of civilization. After a while, he chanced upon a small but shabby house. Exhausted, he got out of the car and knocked on the door. A woman opened the door. He greeted her and explained his situation before asking her if he could use her telephone.

She welcomed him but mentioned that she didn't have a telephone. However, she offered to let him stay till the weather conditions improved. Hungry, wet and exhausted, the doctor accepted her kind offer and walked in.

The hospitable woman served him hot tea and snacks. She offered to pray together. Chuckling, Dr Mark remarked that he only believed in hard work and told her to continue with her prayers.

Seated on a sofa, the doctor watched the woman as she prayed next to a dim candle near what appeared to be a small crib. Every time she finished reading a prayer from the book in front of her, she would begin another verse. He observed that she was in deep meditation.

Sensing that the woman might be in need of help, the doctor seized the opportunity to speak with her as soon as she finished her prayers.

'I saw you deep in prayer,' the doctor broached the topic. 'Do you need help?'

He enquired what exactly she wanted from God and wondered if she thought God would ever listen to her prayers.

'It's my faith,' she asserted. 'I truly believe that He will listen to my prayers.'

'Were you praying for . . .' the doctor asked, pointing to the crib, 'the child? What happened?'

Turning sad, the woman replied, 'Well, that's my son there. And I prayed for him.'

'Anything serious?'

'Yes, he's been diagnosed with a rare type of cancer and I was told there is only one specialist who can cure him. He is not someone I can afford. Plus, he lives in a far-off town, I am told.'

'I see,' the doctor asked. 'What's his name?'

'Dr Mark Austin,' she stated, leaving the doctor stunned.

Speechless, Dr Mark's eyes became moist and he was moved by the gravity of the situation.

Regaining his composure, he whispered to her, 'God is indeed great.'

He walked up to the crib and saw the baby. Then he looked at the altar and said a prayer for two minutes.

Not aware of what was happening and surprised to see the doctor pray, the woman asked, 'But . . .'

'I'm Dr Mark Austin,' he announced, leaving the woman shell-shocked.

The doctor then recollected and narrated the sequence of events to the woman. The malfunctioning of the plane, the thunderstorm that had struck so suddenly, how he lost his way unaware and finally landed here miraculously. The agnostic that he was, he confessed to his change of heart.

'God has indeed answered your sincere prayers,' the doctor comforted her.

She bent down and begged the doctor to help her son.

'Don't you worry,' the doctor assured. 'You have taught me a lesson on behalf of God. To not look for material rewards and possessions but to also invest time to serve poor people who have nothing but rich prayers.'

This story is an amplification of the change of heart in a modern-day leader, who is in the quest for accomplishing more and more, unaware of where he is headed. In the quest to acquire more and more, he is aggravating more and more misery to his deep subconscious self. Let us ponder over certain aspects of bad modern-day leadership and how they disturb mental health.

Highlights of bad modern-day leadership include:

- Feeling alone and threatened make us selfish and cause us to dehumanize others. In the rat race to overtake peers and bosses in order to reach the top, such leaders tend to rub people the wrong way and end up causing mental disturbances not just in others but to their own selves as well. People at the top often miss out on workplace friendships and may suffer mightily as a result. According to a finding in the *Harvard Business Review*, half of the CEOs experience loneliness on the job and most of them feel that loneliness hinders their work performance.[1] Studies also have shown that loneliness is linked to burnout

---

[1] See https://hbr.org/2012/02/its-time-to-acknowledge-ceo-lo#:~:text=Findings%20from%20our%20inaugural%20CEO,particularly%20susceptible%20to%20this%20isolation.

among leaders. One psychologist refers to loneliness as a 'modern epidemic'. Research shows it increases the odds of early death by 20 per cent.[2] To counter this, leaders should become champions of connections. Leaders are at the very centre of nurturing that first connection in particular. Generous leaders develop a gift for making all employees feel a part of that connection and a sense of belonging. Gratitude can complement generosity to build connections, and fight loneliness and isolation.

- Prioritizing the pursuit of profit over all else leads us to dehumanize others. Managing teams just to accomplish financial goals is a myopic leadership style and is short-lived. Today's business setting is miscued in its approach of prioritizing profit over people and the planet. What leaders fail to understand is that they need people (employees, customers, suppliers, etc.) and the planet (natural resources) to acquire profits. Sadly, with their bigoted approach, they ruin relationships

- Scaling of operations makes us think of people as abstractions, consumers, shareholders or expenses. Scaling business further remains an aspiration for most leaders. In that quest, they commoditize the people they are associated with and tend to view them as cheap resources to get work done. They fail to see their human side and are, therefore, unable to tap into the true potential of such meaningful relationships. We are, therefore, more likely to dehumanize others to see them as tools that

---

[2] See https://fortune.com/2016/06/22/loneliness-is-a-modern-day-epidemic/.

fulfil a special purpose, than we are to treat them as living breathing people with their own wants and needs.

- Modern society has become addicted to better and faster performance. Today's society is habituated to everything instant: instant coffee, instant noodles, ready-made chapati, etc. With the development of technology and faster Internet connectivity in the form of the 5G rollout and home delivery of products (through e-commerce) and food, we avail everything faster and at the drop of a hat. Because modern-day people are inured to it, the mind seeks that pace of service and expectations skyrocket and demand programmed or bot-like performance from humans. It's worth noting that addiction is not just for alcohol and drugs; it is also for performance. Better and faster performance in a job is rewarded by the release of dopamine.

For such bad leadership, the message to course correct is: 'Have faith in God, He listens to our prayers. And we should listen to what He is teaching us'.

THIRTY-SEVEN

Offering with Bhakti

Human Quality: Devotion

A sage lived in a hermitage where a lot of students studied under his tutelage. The sage taught and inculcated the principles of Vedic life: svadhyaya (scriptural study), sadhana (practice of devotional service), sadachara (Vaishnava behaviours) and seva (devotional service). With a group of students studying there, sanga (good association) also developed.

The guru was open, transparent and gave daily morning classes from Vedic scriptures like the Bhagavad Gita, *Srimad Bhagavatam*, Itihasas and Puranas. At the end of the class, he always encouraged students to ask questions. His manner of responses was aimed at genuinely making them understand the principles and explaining in detail without any discomfort.

One morning, the sage was speaking on Bhagavad Gita. He explained the verse 9.26,

> *patram puṣpaṁ phalaṁ toyaṁ*
> *yo me bhaktyā prayacchati*
> *tad ahaṁ bhakty-upahṛtam*
> *aśnāmi prayatātmanaḥ*

If one offers Me with love and devotion a leaf, a flower, fruit or water, I will accept it.

The sage shared various pastimes from the Krishna lila episodes of *Srimad Bhagavatam*, of how devotees offered Krishna bhakti, pure love and how such food is sanctified by the Supreme Lord's Grace. Similarly, he also spoke at length about the power of honouring that prasadam, the remnants of the Lord's partaking.

At the end of the class, one student asked a question: 'When we offer food in front of the Lord, does the Lord actually eat that offering?'

The guru responded but the student asked many questions. Since the guru always encouraged them to ask questions and never doubted their intention, the student continued with his repartee. At one point, the guru stopped the discussion and told the student that he would get back to him on this further.

Then, the guru turned to all the disciples and said, 'I want all of you to learn a few mantras.' Then, he gave everybody a book to memorize the mantras. He gave them fifteen minutes to memorize the verse and told them that he would ask them to chant it. The students practised from that book and memorized those mantras.

Fifteen minutes passed and the guru tested the disciples. They all chanted the mantras correctly, including the diction and the emphasis on the gamakam. The guru appreciated the disciples and blessed them all.

Now, the guru asked the student who had questioned him earlier to chant the mantras individually. He chanted them right and effortlessly. The guru praised him.

Very impressed, the guru asked the disciple, 'My dear disciple, did you have to memorize the mantras?'

'Yes, guruji,' the disciple said,

'From where did you learn the mantras?'

'Of course, from the book you gave us.'

'So, did all the mantras from the book enter your mind and thus you memorized them?'

'Yes, guruji,' the student affirmed.

'Can you show me the book?' the guru asked.

The disciple showed him the book.

'Though all the mantras here,' the guru said, pointing to the page in the book, 'have gone into your mind, how are they still printed here?'

The disciple was speechless.

The guru then explained, 'There are two stithis: sthula stithi and sukshma stithi. The text printed here is in sthula stithi (gross form), while the memorized verses that entered your consciousness are in sukshma stithi (subtle form).'

The new concept left the students inspired. The guru had added a new dimension to their learning.

'Likewise, my dear student,' the guru continued, 'when we offer food to Krishna as patram or pushpam or phalam or thoyam, it is in sthula stithi, gross form, while Krishna accepts our kind offering, when offered out of bhakti, in sthula stithi; that is subtle form.'

This new conceptual understanding of spiritual science left the disciple and the entire group stimulated.

The guru concluded saying, 'This is a spiritual transformative process that happens as a result. So, when we partake the remnants of the food accepted by Krishna, that sanctified food transforms us, and nourishes us physically, mentally and spiritually.'

Thankful for the guru's detailed explanation, the disciple prostrated wholeheartedly with his heart pouring gratitude.

Reiterating the verse explained by the guru above, Krishna says in the Gita, 'When one offers with love and devotion (bhakti), leaf, fruit, flour and water, the Lord says I accept it.'

When bhakti enters food, it becomes prasadam,
When bhakti enters hunger, it becomes fasting,
When bhakti enters water, it becomes caranamrita,
When bhakti enters a house, the house
becomes a temple,
When bhakti enters into action, the action
becomes seva,
When bhakti enters into a person, that person
becomes a devotee.

Therefore, let us try to imbibe the principles of bhakti, transform ourselves and become instruments to transform the world that we live in.

In the context of this story, let's analyse the impact of the food that we consume and how we can best leverage the act of eating.

There are three levels of food as per Bhagavad Gita (chapter 17, text 8–10):

- **Food in Mode of Ignorance (tamasic):** These are the foods that make us lazy, dull and lacking vitality in action. Such foods are tamasic in nature and are to be avoided at all costs. Here are some examples of foodstuff in the mode of ignorance:

o eaten more than three hours after preparation
o tasteless
o decomposed
o putrid
o remnants
o untouchable things

- **Food in Mode of Passion (rajas):** These are those foods that incite passion in us and leads us to becoming angry, lusty and greedy. They tend to make the mind crave for and drive into a mad hankering after pursuits without sense control or any sort of regulated behaviour. Such foods in the mode of passion are:

o too bitter
o too sour
o too salty
o too hot/spicy
o too pungent
o too dry and burning
o cause distress, misery and disease

- **Food in Mode of Goodness (satvik):** These are high-quality and fresh foods that energize the mind and nourish the body, mind and soul. They infuse physical vitality into the body, supply positivity and a sense of clarity to the mind. When such food in goodness is offered to God with pure love and affection, it transforms from being satvik to shuddh satvik (prasadam). This prasadam is accepted graciously by God and He partakes it. When we honour the remnants of prasadam, it replenishes the soul with divinity and uplifts our consciousness to better serve God and people around us. Such food in the mode of goodness:

o   increases the duration of life
o   purify one's existence
o   gives strength, health, happiness and satisfaction
o   is juicy, fatty, wholesome and pleasing to the heart

THIRTY-EIGHT

The Caged Parrot

Human Quality: Wisdom

Once upon a time, Sheela, a college student, went to the market to purchase a parrot in a cage. She chose the parrot of her choice, with wings and a body of the most beautiful colours. The bird had a curved beak and zygodactyl feet (meaning each foot had four toes, with two facing forward and two facing backward). Such feet, as they gave birds the ability to manipulate things well with their feet, were very attractive. She attached as much importance to the cage as well and selected one. She also ensured that a fine balance was maintained between caging the bird and viewing it from outside. The student considered it a prized possession and brought it home excitedly.

She kept admiring the beauty of the new entrant. Moreover, she wanted to decorate the cage further and amplify its beauty. First, she took a brush and cleaned the cage diligently. She painted the cage in fine colours, complementing the bird. She brought some mirrors and placed them inside the cage so that the parrot could look at the mirrors and feel good about itself. She brought some bells and hung them around the cage. When the wind would blow, she wanted the sound of the bells to reverberate in the air melodiously.

Despite her best efforts, in a couple of days, she found the parrot lying on the floor of the cage. It just would not respond to any of her calls. She became frantic and went to the person who sold her the parrot.

'Look at this parrot,' Sheela exclaimed. 'I'm making all kinds of arrangements for the parrot, but somehow it is not responding.'

'That's strange!' the owner responded. 'May I know what all did you do with the parrot?'

'Well, I decorated the cage basically; cleaned the cage, painted it, made it shine, added bells to it and so on.'

'This looks nice,' the man praised her. 'But, did you feed the parrot, madam?'

'Well, that I didn't do,' Sheela realized her mistake.

This message in this story is akin to someone fuelling the car but not feeding the driver. Such a practice is a superficial outlook towards life, with a bodily basis without caring for the soul, the atma. Our temporary identity is defined in the relationships we forge with someone or something. With changes in our name, residence, occupation, religion and gender, our temporary identity also changes. All our temporary identities are based on the premise that we are our bodies. Our permanent identity is that we are the spirit soul, a living spark that resides within the body. The body and soul are like a cage and a parrot, an apartment and a resident, and a car and a driver respectively.

In this world, each one of us live in five conditions of nescience or ignorance which are as follows:

- **Tamah:** Forgetful of one's real identity as an eternal soul and unaware of the nature and purpose of existence, one doesn't enquire about life and the vicious cycle of birth and death that grips every living being. One just goes about life and similar to animals, focuses energy on the basic necessities of life—eating, sleeping, mating and defending. In this mode of forgetfulness, without making the basic enquiries of life, one leads life of animalistic propensities in the mode of ignorance.

- **Moham:** False identification with one's temporary body under illusion and under the mode of ignorance, one identifies with the body that one has. There are multiple identities that one forms based on different categories like gender (male/female), nationality (American/Australian/Indian/Russian), age category (boy/youth/old), skin complexion (fair/dark/wheatish), race (Caucasian/Asian/Black) and so on. One continues to believe in such temporary identification and leads a life swamped in illusion.

- **Mahamoham:** Due to a false sense of ownership and proprietorship of things offered by arrangement of superior control in the mode of passion, one claims complete ownership and belongingness to temporary possession of things and relationships in the world: my house, my car, my mobile phone, my bike, etc. Such an arrangement of these temporary possessions has been kindly bestowed on us by God out of His mercy and in recognition of the past good karma (punya). The real understanding that one should cultivate is that each and everything in this world belongs to God completely. Right from a speck of mud on the ground and the huts to the beautiful villas, the tallest skyscrapers to the moon and the sun that illuminate the world, these are all a part and parcel of God. They manifest due to God's energy. God has kindly granted us to temporarily use an infinitesimal portion of His wealth in the form of the beautiful family that we are born into, the wonderful house that we live in, the comfortable cars that we drive in, the wealth that we generate in our business, so on and so forth. They all remain with us until we are in the body. Once we (the soul) depart from our respective bodies, we lose possession of them.

- **Tamisram:** When one's plan for ownership and enjoyment is frustrated by the time factor and the balloon of thinking 'I am great' is punctured by the circumstances facilitated by the time factor, one becomes angry. Time can be both a healer and teacher. It just depends on the context and the perspective with which we view time. Everything in this world has a shelf life. The most charming of actors cannot remain the hero/heroine in movies beyond a certain age, the fastest of athletes are gold medallists for a much shorter duration in their youth, the most charismatic of politicians lead for a shorter duration (four to five years) and then need to run for office again. However, if one were to think that their hold/ownership over their titles and enjoyment of success is permanent (lusty) while the time factor proves otherwise, the unfulfilled lust becomes anger.

- **Andhatamisram:** Finally, time, the ultimate frustrater of all plans, manifests as death to create fear in the conditioned soul's heart, when the prospect of enjoyer and controllership is destroyed. Unfulfilled lust becomes anger, while fulfilled lust becomes greed. As one tastes success in accomplishing something, one wants to leverage on it and seeks to acquire more and more, as per the directions of the mind. That is greed. As a result of past good karma and the beneficiary time factor, one can accumulate more and more. However, time manifests as death to wipe away any sort of proprietorship over anything in this world.

To summarize, Krishna says in the Bhagavad Gita (2.20),

na jāyate mriyate vā kadācin
nāyaṁ bhūtvā bhavitā vā na bhūyaḥ
ajo nityaḥ śāśvato 'yaṁ purāṇo
na hanyate hanyamāne śarīre

The soul is within this body, which is like a cage, and the soul cannot be destroyed in any situation. And therefore, the soul needs to be nourished on a regular basis. In this age of kali, the means to nourish the soul is by the power of the chanting of the holy names, Hare Krishna Hare Krishna Krishna Krishna Hare Hare Hare Rama Hare Rama Rama Rama Hare Hare. If we simply take care of the cage (body), and forget the parrot (soul), then we miss the central point. As discussed earlier, the driver of the car must be in the best state of mind for the journey to be safe. Fuelling the car alone won't suffice. And yes, the body must be taken care of, but we should not forget to take care of the soul within. The soul is eternal while the body is temporary. Nourishing the soul within this cage of the body and moving closer to God is the real purpose of the human form of life.

THIRTY-NINE

Dare to Dream

Human Quality: Ambition

Along the shores of Salinas in California lived Monty Roberts, the teenage son of a horse trainer, in a humble house. His father had to move from farm to farm, ranch to ranch, training horses in the city. The city was a tourist destination for horse riding. What the father made was just enough to make ends meet for the family.

One day in school, Monty was asked by his teacher to write a weekend essay on the topic, 'My Dream in Life'. Monty wrote a seven-page essay that weekend, where he detailed his dream of having a huge ranch with several horses, the superior structure of stables, food transportation for the horses, the training mechanism to be adopted for the horses, the design features, etc. It was literally a detailed blueprint of his plan, which he believed would not just be a guide for his life but also take horse-riding tourism in Walvis Bay to the next level. What he had learned from his father, what he had seen him do at work, what he had observed in his father's interactions with others in the business and some of his own realizations came to the fore as he produced an in-depth picture of his dream vividly.

Monty felt very happy with what he had put together with deep thought. He felt this was something he could live by after his formal education. That Monday morning, he submitted the essay. Two days later, the teacher returned the paper with an F. Monty was taken aback. Reality was poles apart as far as his expectations were concerned. He just couldn't accept it and, in a sense, felt that his dreams were shattered. Deeply disturbed by the grade, he approached the teacher and requested an explanation.

The teacher looked at the paper and said, 'You've failed.'

'I know, ma'am,' Monty replied, shocked. 'But I wrote such an elaborate essay on my dreams in life.'

'Your dreams are unrealistic,' she snapped. 'You have no land or property. Today, you are wandering from ranch to ranch. And, you've written that you are going to have several thousand acres of ranch and several hundred horses. It just doesn't make sense.'

'Ma'am, but I'll . . .'

'Go home, Monty,' the teacher remarked. 'Edit this paper and come back with a more realistic essay.'

Dejected, Monty went home that evening and sobbed. Noticing that his son was low in spirits, his father sat next to him, comforted him and asked him for details. Monty explained the details and shared the essay that he had written.

His father read the seven-page essay patiently.

'It's so well-written, Monty,' he praised him. 'You've applied your full knowledge of horse-riding tourism in this part of the country. Wonderful!'

'But my teacher has asked me to edit it.'

'Well, you have a choice. Either you live with this dream, or you edit it. The choice is yours.'

Inspired and believing in his dream, Monty went back with the seven-page essay, handed it back to his teacher and said, 'My dear teacher, I will keep the dream and you keep the grades with you.'

Today, Monty Roberts owns a 4000-square-foot house on a 200-acre ranch and trains hundreds of horses there.

What an inspiring story of continuous self-improvement, which is a function of willpower. As they say, 'where there is a will, there is a way', and that will leads to self-improvement when powered by determination and discrimination.

To increase willpower, we need to focus on two areas:

- **Discrimination:** Capacity to differentiate between the following is important:
  o **The Harmful and Beneficial:** The intelligence powers the mind with the ability to discriminate. Hence, it's important we feed the intelligence with authorized sources of knowledge. Besides the five gross senses, the three subtle senses are made up of the mind, intelligence and false ego. Intelligence is the powerhouse of intellect and drives the mind, and false ego is based on the knowledge that we gather and store. Accordingly, it helps discriminate between what is favourable and unfavourable for progress.
  o **The Short Term and the Long Term:** When we are led by well-informed personalities who have derived knowledge from authorized sources, the mind is

balanced to discriminate between short-term and long-term pleasures. Sometimes, we are lured by the temptations of the world that give fleeting pleasure but are actually not conducive to long-term progress. The short-term pleasures, in the garb of happiness, misdirect us and are short-lived. They make us lose direction. A well-thought-out approach would be to pursue goals for the long term.

- **Determination:** The strength to act as per our determination is important:

  o **To Accept the Beneficial Even If It Is Temporarily Painful:** Every morning when our alarm goes off at, say, 5 a.m., we are faced with a decision: 'Do I get up and deal with the temporary pain and discomfort of getting up?' or 'Do I stay in bed and live with the regret on my mind all day?' The willingness to sacrifice and suffer from temporary pain in order to gain long-term pleasure is not something that's built into humans naturally. That's because we have been conditioned in a certain way. However, with determination, as we pursue it assiduously and shackle the temptations of the mind, we reap the desired results. Over time, we realize that the long-term benefits of getting up early greatly surpass the pain of those first few minutes of actually getting up.

  o **To Eschew Harmful Habits Even If They Are Temporarily Pleasurable:** When we know that doing something is bad, why can't we just stop doing it? It's said that although most alcoholics would like to quit drinking, they struggle to do so as it hurts them both physically and mentally. Moving on to physical fitness, many of us have unhealthy or excess weight that we could lose if only we eat right and exercise more.

Enjoyable behaviours (like drinking a glass of liquor or eating an extra sweet or indulging in cheesy foodstuff) prompt the brain to release a chemical called dopamine. When we repeat a certain activity and it becomes a habit, dopamine is there when we indulge in it. That strengthens the habit further. When we stay away from these activities, dopamine creates the craving to do it again. But we human beings are not simply creatures of habit with animalistic propensities. We have many more regions in the brain that help us do what is best for our health. This is where willpower plays an important role in overcoming such enticement.

The secret of unswerving determination is the alignment of the human will with the divine will.

Determination is the psychology of success in any field. The quality of our determination dictates the quality of our life. The three building blocks of determination are:

- **Philosophy:** Knowledge is like a sword which cuts our doubts and builds our convictions. The purpose behind our actions feeds the intelligence with a number of choices.
- **People:** An African proverb says: 'If you want to walk fast, walk alone; if you want to walk far, walk with many'.[1]

---

[1] See https://www.npr.org/sections/goatsandsoda/2016/07/30/487925796/
it-takes-a-village-to-determine-the-origins-of-an-african-proverb.

- **Practice:** Regular movement is more important than prolonged planning and contemplating. The secret of unleashing the power of determination is to overcome the inertia to 'start'.

And so, it is said that we should always have the determination to be able to dream about what we want to do. As described by Lord Krishna in Bhagavad Gita (2.41),

> *vyavasāyātmikā buddhir*
> *ekeha kuru-nandana*
> *bahu-śākhā hy anantāś ca*
> *buddhayo 'vyavasāyinām*

Any kind of successful activity in the material or in the spiritual world requires determination, focus and single-minded effort. Let's try to accomplish that and make our life successful.

Success requires focused determination.

FORTY

The Scientist and the Bhagavad Gita[1]

Human Quality: Humility

Ajay, a young man, had just graduated as a scientist. To fulfil his dream, he applied for and successfully secured a job at the Bhabha Atomic Research Centre. He landed in Thiruvananthapuram one afternoon. That evening, he was strolling along the shores of the beach. At a distance, he noticed an elderly gentleman seated and immersed in reading a book. He walked closer. As he reached the bench that the gentleman was seated on, he observed that the man was reading the Bhagavad Gita.

An agnostic, young Ajay, enthused after having landed his dream job, gathered the courage to begin a conversation, 'Sir, may I know what you are reading?'

'The Bhagavad Gita,' the elderly man said with a smile and offered Ajay a place to sit on the bench.

'But, why are you wasting your time reading the Gita?' asked Ajay out of mild arrogance.

---

[1] Adapted from *Vikram Sarabhai: A Life* by Amrita Shah, published by Penguin Books India, New Delhi, in 2007.

'Well, I'm very much fascinated by the mystery here,' the elderly man said, clearing his throat. 'There is a lot in here, you should consider reading it too someday.'

'Sir, there is no point reading such outdated literature. I'm sorry to say but you're simply wasting your time.'

The elderly man remained silent.

'And if you are from a scientific background,' Ajay added affirmatively, 'then this has absolutely no relevance. I am a scientist and so I can say that ultimately all the answers are in science. There is no point studying the Gita.'

The old man smiled and asked, 'Well, young man, what is your background? And what's your profession?'

'Well, I am a scientist and I'm joining the Bhabha Atomic Research Centre tomorrow.'

'Well, congratulations,' the man praised him.

A car suddenly appeared there at that moment. With a beacon flashing on the top, it seemed like a car reserved for a high official in the Government of India.

'Well, I have to go now,' the elderly man said. 'I wish you all the best.' With those parting words, he got up and started walking towards the car. Ajay was surprised and curious to know who this gentleman was.

'Sir,' he called out.

'Yes, boy, tell me,' the man looked back.

Ajay walked a few paces towards the man and asked, 'Who are you, sir? I can't recognize you.'

The elderly man said, 'My name is Dr Vikram Sarabhai.'

Ajay was speechless. The elderly man tapped on his shoulder gently. Ajay was bewildered because this was the person who headed the Bhabha Atomic Research Centre at that time. He was the chairperson of the Atomic Energy Commission.

Just as Dr Sarabhai proceeded to the car, Ajay requested him for a minute.

'Sir, you're such a such an eminent scientist. Why are you studying the Gita? May I know?'

Dr Sarabhai smiled at him and said, 'Well, if, as scientists we are fascinated by creation, I am simply trying to understand the mystery of the Creator and there is no better book to understand the mystery of the Creator then this Bhagavad Gita.'

Lord Krishna says in the Bhagavad Gita (10.8),

> *aham sarvasya prabhavo*
> *mattah sarvam pravartate*
> *iti matvā bhajante mām*
> *budhā bhāva-samanvitāh*

I am the ultimate creator, the source of all spiritual and material worlds. Everything emanates from Me. The wise who perfectly know this worship Me with all their hearts.

This emphatic statement by Krishna should put to rest any speculation about the creator and the source of all knowledge, including the need of the hour of this timeless scripture, the Bhagavad Gita. However, unfortunately, modern society is enchanted by external success while the ancient Vedic society prioritized internal success. Let's delve into these accidental misplaced priorities and how we can correct them for the better.

Modern society's idea of external success consists of the following:

- **Penny:** As they say, 'money is honey'. People think that accumulating wealth is the be-all and end-all of happiness. They fail to understand that it comes with restrictions. A happiness study of nations conducted in 2017 found that a lot of countries in sub-Saharan Africa, although poor, fared well in it.[2]

- **Position:** Often, we ask children in school, 'What do you want to become when you grow up?' That leads the children to think on the lines of taking a certain position in life, like that of a CEO, prime minister, district collector, astronaut, etc. There's nothing wrong in having aspirations but such a line of thought limits them. As opposed to becoming something or taking on a certain position, children should be encouraged to think on values and the character they need to develop. When values are instilled correctly, everything else, including position, are byproducts and are taken care of.

- **Power:** Ephemeral success in the garb of power enchants people. In olden times, people saw power as a source of responsibility and strived to live up to it when handed over the mandate of a certain power centre. However, today, power is misused and sometimes even abused to settle personal scores or to heighten a certain individual's stature in society. They fail to understand the reality

---

[2] See https://qz.com/africa/1175189/pew-research-on-happy-africans-story-is-much-more-complex-than-we-thought/.

that power is associated with a certain position that is temporarily held by a certain individual to execute a certain responsibility.

- **Popularity:** As with many things in life, popularity is more complicated than it appears to be. The people in the first category are popular because they are likable—their peers like them for who they are, trust them and want to associate with them. The second category is made of people who become popular because they somehow gain a certain status and use that power to wield influence over others. People who seek to be likable can potentially end up living a healthier life, partake in meaningful relationships, pursue more fulfilling work and live longer. The status seekers, though, often end up anxious and depressed, and with addiction problems. In the age of social media, driven by likes, loves and other emotions, the mind is titillated and hence gravitates to the wrong type of popularity.

- **Possessions:** Temporary acquisition of a certain wealth, power, position or a commodity is seen as possession in this modern age. At its core, people identify with it, seek to claim proprietorship and become attached to it. Beauty, wealth and good health are certain gifts of God that need to make people grateful but due to their misdirected knowledge, they lay permanent claim to it. However, the time factor shows people what the ground reality is. The famous last words of Alexander the Great are: 'Bury my body, do not build any monument, keep my hands outside so that the world knows the person who won the world had nothing in his hands when dying.'[3]

Modern civilization forces us to lead lives based on hurry and worry:

- **Hurry:** We are in a fast mode to get things done and to cope with our to-do list. The mode of passion is prominent in this.
- **Worry:** The anxiety of experiencing the gap between expectation and reality makes us take shelter under activities to distract our mind. These activities include entertainment, addictions, etc. The mode of ignorance impels this.

However, the seekers of wisdom follow the path of mode of goodness, focusing on priority and divinity.

- **Priority:** The mode of goodness creates purity and clarity in our consciousness. One is able to choose his desires for long-term benefit.
- **Divinity:** When our desires are controlled, we rise above the material and experience divinity, which gives us a taste of transcendental service.

---

[3] See https://www.leader.co.za/article.aspx?s=1&f=1&a=4225#:~:text=I%20 want%20my%20hands%20to,exhausted%2C%20and%20that%20is%20 TIME and https://www.scrolldroll.com/quotes-by-alexander-the-great/.

FORTY-ONE

The Powerful Mango

Human Quality: Humility

Shivaji, an old man living in the temple town of Kolhapur, had two sons, Vijay and Sujay. At his deathbed, Shivaji called his sons and said, 'Sorry, I led a normal life and was not able to accumulate wealth. I have nothing to leave behind for you. But, out of love, I give you this mango. Please share it among yourselves.'

The elder son, Vijay, snatched the mango and didn't care to offer even a piece to his younger brother, Sujay. He took it all for himself and his wife. Once they enjoyed it, so as to annoy Sujay, Vijay took the seed that remained. With great impudence, he threw it across the fence into Sujay's courtyard.

'Did you see the seed?' Vijay sneered. 'That's my gift to you.'

The parents advised Vijay to not fight and asked him to maintain his composure at such a critical time in his father's life. Sujay didn't complain, said soft words to his father and prayed for him. Shivaji breathed his last soon and passed away in a few moments.

Later that afternoon, Sujay went home, picked up that seed, washed it with humility and with great care planted it in a small pot. He carefully tended it for days. Gradually, as the sapling grew, he took it out of the pot and placed it at a strategic location in his backyard where he would need shade in the future. He would regularly worship and take care of the mango plant, till it became a huge, luxuriant and beautiful mango tree. Over time, it became an orchard, providing all kinds of luxuriant fruits.

What appeared to be waste was carefully picked up and cared for, and eventually grew into a giant tree, a source of great benefit.

How often in life do we find ourselves in Sujay's shoes? As in this story, life throws us into a situation where we feel that we are not treated fairly, where we are not given the love and the affection that we would otherwise shower on others and where we are frowned upon. It's also worth introspecting how we respond to such situations. One of the deepest and widely applicable lessons from the Bhagavad Gita is that 'we have limited control over the circumstances that we are put into but we have unlimited control over the consciousness with which we respond to them'. Srila Prabhupada, the Founder Acharya of ISKCON, often remarked that the greatness of a person lies in the ability to tolerate provoking situations. What we observed in this story was indeed a provoking situation, but the younger brother exhibited composure, showed tolerance and chose to see an opportunity in the seed that was thrown. In short, what he displayed was civilized behaviour.

In the *Srimad Bhagavatam* (1.9.26), Shri Bhishmadeva advises Yudhiṣṭhira maharaja about the nine qualities that make a person civilized,

> *puruṣa-sva-bhāva-vihitān*
> *yathā-varṇaṁ yathāśramam*
> *vairāgya-rāgopādhibhyām*
> *āmnātobhaya-lakṣaṇān*

- **Overcoming Anger:** Anger, as they say, is one letter short of danger. The Bhagavad Gita explains that from anger, complete delusion arises, and from delusion, bewilderment of memory. When the memory is bewildered, intelligence is lost, and when intelligence is lost, one falls down again into the material pool. That one momentary spurt of emotions can wreak havoc on the mental health of a person. When two people are angry at each other, their hearts grow distant. To cover that distance, they must shout to be able to hear each other. The angrier they are, the louder they will have to shout to hear each other through that great distance. A civilized person understands the ramification of an agitated mind and as a result, controls any outburst of emotions or rage that ensues.
- **Renounce Speaking Lies:** In the context of lying, there is an interesting note from the *Srimad Bhagavatam* (8.20.4): There is nothing more sinful than untruthfulness. Because of this, Mother Earth once said, 'I can bear any heavy thing except a person who is a liar.' It is said that on

the surface of the earth there are many great mountains and oceans that are very heavy, and Mother Earth has no difficulty carrying them. A civilized person is grateful for what Mother Earth showers upon us and always speaks the truth.

- **Equitable Wealth Distribution:** A civilized person remains fair in dealings and is not greedy. Such a person understands that everything in this world is the property of God. As a result, righteously, they take their share of the pie and serve those who need help. Such a person shows deep empathy and wants to positively impact people.

- **Forgiveness:** Forgiveness is understood as a deliberate choice to release feelings of anger, resentment or vengeance towards a person who has offended us, without considering whether the offender deserves our forgiveness. By forgiving someone, we make the decision to stop judging the person who harmed us and let go the expectation of even an apology. Replacing negative emotions and the desire to punish the transgressor, we express compassion and kindness. For most of us, this art does not come naturally and the task of forgiveness takes some inner work. As we consciously pursue it, we enhance our civility index. Research on the benefits of forgiveness on health and longevity reveals that forgiveness is positively correlated with stronger circulatory and immune systems. Psychologically speaking, people who forgive more willingly are less likely to be depressed and anxious and more likely to be happy. These merits of forgiveness seem to forecast a longer, more pleasant life. Our response to personal insult has a lasting effect on our well-being.

- **To Beget Children from One's Legitimate Wife:** In a Vedic civilization, sex life is allowed but regulated. It is sanctioned for a married couple but only for the purpose of begetting children. A civilized person never indulges in sexual affairs outside of marriage. More so, even within marriage, sex life is not indulged in for the purpose of sense gratification. Because they know well that should they commit, both the man and the woman await severe reactions from it. A civilized person begets children within the institution of marriage and raises them as socially, morally and spiritually responsible citizens.

- **To Be Pure in Mind and Hygienic in Body:** Purity is an important aspect of being a civilized human. Not only does it create an environment conducive to the development of clear consciousness, but it is an integral part of spiritual development. Purity is reflected in the cleanliness adopted. A clean person makes a clean home, and that, when combined, becomes a clean society and then a clean nation and finally a cleaner world. Cleanliness involves both internal and external aspects. One remains pure by adopting a spiritual lifestyle. This includes firm faith in God, chanting the names of the Lord and offering prayers to Him regularly, systematically studying the scriptures, following scriptural rules and regulations, respecting authority and engaging in devotional service, all of which helps us manage the agitated mind.

- **Not To Be Inimical towards Anyone:** A civilized person's consistent practice of purity clears the mind of impurities accumulated over lifetimes and enables them to discriminate between the good and the bad. It also helps them to view the world through new eyes, without anger, greed, envy or enmity. A civilized person with such a clean mind is able to remain stable and forge healthy relationships with not only those around them but with God as well.

- **To Be Simple:** A civilized person follows the motto: simple living and high thinking. Simplicity means without duplicity. Such a person who is simple has no ulterior motives. They speak honestly and politely to encourage others. Such a person with simplicity of mind has simplicity of lifestyle, which means that they are detached from gain or loss, pleasure or pain, honour or dishonour, happiness or distress. They simply seek purification of the consciousness and exhibit civility in behaviour.

- **To Support Servants and Subordinates:** Such a civilized person takes no one for granted. They see every person as a part and parcel of God, beyond the bodily aspects visible to the naked eye and can appreciate people for who they are. They cultivate relationships with servants as they see an opportunity to serve them and, in that process, purify their own consciousness.

FORTY-TWO

The World Does Not Stop

Human Quality: Modesty

There was once a man in a village who headed a family that comprised his mother, wife and two children. Raised in a lower-middle-class family, he worked hard and had great confidence in his abilities. As the only breadwinner, he maintained his family well and raised their comforts over a period. Since he felt that he single-handedly protected his family, there was an associated pride that took birth in his mind. The man was well-respected in the village as he behaved well with one and all and contributed to the affairs of the village by participating in social activities. He was not a believer of God and preached to people to only believe in their abilities and hard work.

The village had a practice of organizing daily Hari katha in the morning. It was the norm for residents to attend. However, the non-believer that he was, the man never attended the lectures. One morning, a prominent saint visited the village and kindly accepted the invitation to talk on Srimad Bhagavad Gita. Waiting to hear from the saint, a huge crowd arrived. As the katha was going on, the man had to walk past the massive crowd on his way to work. As he was passing by, he had to hear the katha. Although uninterested, the words of the speaker involuntarily entered his ears.

The saint was speaking thus: 'Everything in this world happens by the will of Krishna and therefore, ultimately, whether we expect a certain thing or not, even if we are present or not present to perform the activities, things will go on as per the will of God. We are insignificant and act as mere instruments of God.'

As the man heard these words, they enraged him. As someone who took pride in the fact that he worked hard for his family, maintained them and led from the front, he became furious. More so, he felt it was he who led events in his family and he believed that affairs in the family revolved around him. He wanted to challenge the saint right away. However, his gentlemanly behaviour came to the fore. Considering the katha was going on for a large audience, he kept quiet and avoided creating a chaos there. But he definitely wanted to raise the issue with the saint and waited for the right opportunity. Since he was getting late for work, he made his way to his office.

However, throughout the forenoon, he was deeply disturbed by the katha. Those were powerful and heartbreaking words, he thought. They pricked him and the hard worker that he was, he wasn't in his element that day. He felt offended and couldn't bear to sit there beyond lunch. He applied for leave that afternoon, left office and walked straight to the house where the saint was present.

He didn't offer respects and expressed his displeasure right away, 'How dare you speak such words this morning?'

'Ji? May I know who you are?' the seer politely asked. 'Please can you explain what help you need.'

'I need no help from you,' the man continued in anger. 'I heard your morning talk. How could you say that we are insignificant and that things will go on by the will of God?'

The saint got a sense of where the man was coming from and the reason for his rage.

'If I'm not there,' the man added in contempt, 'who will protect my mother and wife? Who will take care of my son? Who will take care of my daughter? My son doesn't have a job and my daughter has not yet gotten married. We are unable to find her a partner. I work so hard and you, old man, just sit on a chair and lecture people on nonsense.'

'I wish you well,' the seer blessed him.

'I don't need your blessings. I don't believe in this. Take back your words and apologize.'

'Not required. Things go on in this world by the will of Krishna. We are mere instruments.'

'Don't you dare repeat these words!' the man thundered. 'I have to be here to do all of it. How will things in my family happen without me? If I'm not present, everything will stop in my family.'

'I see,' the saint sighed. 'I give you a challenge.'

'What challenge?'

'Why don't you go absconding for a year? Then, we'll see whether things actually go on or not.'

'Don't blabber, I'll not leave.'

'Then, you accept becoming the instrument of God for your family. My point is that even without you, things will go on as per the will of God.'

'No, I don't accept this point of view.'

'Then, accept the challenge and see for yourself,' the seer dared him.

The man thought for a minute. To keep his head high, he accepted the challenge. He was keen to prove the saint wrong.

'Okay, fine,' the man confirmed. 'What should I do now?'

'That's good,' the saint nodded. 'You come and stay with me in my village. I will keep you in a secluded space. I will manage the communication with your family.'

The man agreed but warned, 'I don't want you to be involved in the affairs of my family beyond communicating to them about me absconding.'

'For sure, son,' the saint confirmed.

As agreed, the man stayed in a secluded place and didn't return to his home for a year. The agent of the saint communicated to his family that the man died in an accident and the body went missing following the tragedy. Bewildered, the family was left shattered. They just couldn't come to terms with this sudden turn of events. As time passed, the man didn't want to be away from his family. He didn't want to spend the time alone or not do anything. But he persisted for a year just to keep his word and to challenge the saint. A year passed and he walked up to the saint.

'It is time for me to go back to my family,' the man said to the saint.

'Thank you for keeping up your word. I appreciate it.'

'You have lost the challenge, sir,' the man smirked at the saint.

'It's not yet over, son,' the saint smiled. 'Go and meet your family. You will know who won and who lost.'

Though confused and keen to debate with the saint, the man was desperate to meet his family after a year. He went back to his family. As he entered, he found that the family was happy and leading a normal life, as always. That shook the man. Moments later, as the family members saw the man enter the house, they were astounded.

'Ghost, ghost,' the son cried.

It took a while for the man to explain the situation. They bonded for a while and there was euphoria in the house. They were thrilled to see him back. Just then, the man realized that the daughter was missing. He enquired about her.

'She got married,' the wife said with mixed feelings. While she was happy that the daughter was married, she regretted that her husband had not been there at that time.

'What?' the man exclaimed. Shocked, he fell on the sofa.

'Yes, in fact, when the news of your death reached us, Virdas, one of the most powerful merchants in the village, offered his son's hand in marriage for our daughter. They were happy with whatever we could spend on the marriage and graciously accepted her.'

The man was taken aback. It felt like his heart was bludgeoned. His ego was crushed.

'Yes, dad,' the son said. 'At the wedding, I met with a businessman, who is the bridegroom's maternal uncle. He offered me a job so that I could earn for the family.'

'It was God's grace,' the man's mother delivered the knockout punch, 'that even though you were not around, everything happened well.'

Speechless, the man prostrated in front of the altar. He acknowledged his vanity and humbly submitted to the statue of Krishna in his home. Right away that evening, he paid a visit to the saint along his family and repented for his mistakes.

In this regard, there is a beautiful verse in the *Srimad Bhagavatam* (1.13.46).

kāla-karma-guṇādhīno
deho 'yaṁ pāñca-bhautikaḥ
katham anyāṁs tu gopāyet
sarpa-grasto yathā param

It is said herein that under the influence of kala, karma and guna, which is time, activity and the modes of nature, things are moving and therefore, it is only out of false pride that a person thinks that they are the doer.

One needs to take due steps to remove false pride to get rid of the doer mentality. If we dig deep into the basics of the Bhagavad Gita, we understand and realize that we are not independent but totally dependent on God.

Two key means by which one can overcome false pride is through:

- **Knowledge of One's Real Identity:** If we get back to the Gita fundamentals, we recognize that we are not this body but spirit soul, part and parcel of Krishna. Qualitatively, we are one and the same, but quantitatively, we are an infinitesimally small as compared to Krishna. When we cultivate this correct understanding and feed this into our subconscious mind, we remain humble and there is no room for false pride in our day-to-day behaviour.

- **Awareness of the All-powerful Time Factor:** Further, Gita fundamentals also describe the temporary nature of the body that we inhabit and the temporary nature of the world that we live in. Even if we are materially successful and accumulate massive amounts of wealth, attain an important status in society and have a huge following of people, these are temporary and are wiped to nothing at the time of death. While yes, the death knell is final, there are also times in life when wealth is wiped off instantly. The volatility of the stock market erodes a million dollars of wealth in a single day. In today's age of social media-influenced financial markets, a business magnate's single tweet can spike the market cap of a stock, while on the flip side it can also erode billions. In early 2021, due to a single tweet, Tesla CEO Elon Musk lost $15 billion on a single day.[1] That's a sign of the precariousness of the times that we live in.

For one who is proud and egoistic, the all-powerful time snatches away all the so-called possessions that one was proud of. While every material relationship is temporary, our spiritual relationship with Krishna as His servant is permanent. In such a humble attitude of service, we can overcome false pride and get rid of the doership mentality.

According to the *Chanakya Niti* (CN 12.11), our six eternal family relationships are as follows:

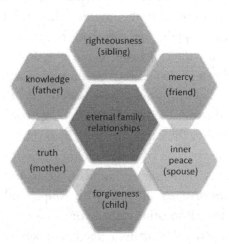

---

1 See https://www.livemint.com/companies/people/elon-musk-loses-world-s-richest-title-one-tweet-costs-him-15-billion-11614066047519.html.

FORTY-THREE

Knowledge Precedes Action

Human Quality: Wisdom

At the Boston harbour, a container ship was about to start its voyage. The vessel's capacity was 20,000 twenty-foot equivalent unit (TEU). Its length was over 300 metres and breadth over 50 metres. It was scheduled to travel across the Atlantic Ocean into Africa and Europe.

The captain started the engine. Suddenly, there was a sputtering sound and the engine failed right away. That bemused the captain, as this had been a planned effort spanning many days of loading and preparing the ship. He spoke to the technicians on the ship and they were yet to figure out what was going on. Suddenly, at the harbour, a middle-aged man noticed what was going on.

He talked to the captain, 'Can I help you?'

'Who are you and what do you know about ship engines?'

'Captain, I am a marine engineer,' he assured the captain. 'I have extensive experience with ships and I am now consulting for automotive engine companies.'

Convinced, the captain agreed to take his help. They mutually agreed that this would be a paid service.

Before a major breakdown could ensue, the engineer intervened. He opened his tool box, took a hammer and then went right next to the engine. There, he began inspecting the engine carefully. He spent a good fifteen minutes there.

At one particular spot, he struck the engine with the hammer.

Right away, he told the captain, 'Start the engine now.'

The captain started the engine. It was smooth, without any noise.

Ecstatic, the captain thanked the engineer, 'Wow, you are a genius. With one strike of the hammer, you made the engine work.'

'Thank .you,' the engineer said, and handed over an invoice for $2000.

Looking at the bill, the smile fell from the captain's face.

Bewildered, the captain raised his voice, 'What is this nonsense? You just took a hammer and hit the hammer on the engine. That's about it.'

Unfazed, the engineer responded, 'That's right.'

'Why have you charged a whopping $2000 for this?'

'Captain, $2 for hammering and $1998 to figure out where to hammer. That's the power of knowledge.'

In the Bhagavad Gita (8.7), Krishna says,

> *tasmāt sarveṣu kāleṣu*
> *mām anusmara yudhya ca*
> *mayy arpita-mano-buddhir*
> *mām evaiṣyasy asaṁśayaḥ*

At all times, remember me. And if you fight with that understanding, you will come to me without fail.

The Gita does not promote inaction, but it promotes meditative action. And therefore, Krishna inspired Arjuna to take the actions with the right consciousness. The right action is not simply in moving the hands and legs but, just like the man with the hammer, we need to know what to think, how to think and which direction to think in while performing the action. That's the million-dollar question and the answer is here in the Gita. Let us dive deep into it further.

The Bhagavad Gita defines knowledge as knowing matter, spirit and controller of both. It uses three metaphors to describe transcendental knowledge (jnana):

- Jnana-agni or the Fire of Knowledge: The purpose of karma is not to inflict random suffering but to educate us about the purpose behind pain. When we encounter a certain pain in life, we must immediately understand that it is due to a previously committed sin and as a result, we experience a certain pain now. There is no need to develop a certain complex but just objectively understand the purpose of it and karma as a concept applicable eternally—past, present and future.

- When one views such experiences through the lens of knowledge, one makes choices accordingly with the right understanding of karma. As it is said, 'pain is compulsory, suffering is optional'. One doesn't get bogged down by the pain but understands it in the context of the larger scheme of things. As a result, one doesn't lament but accepts the pain as an opportunity to think of Krishna, seek His guidance and refrain from committing any more sin and make better choices in life.

- Such knowledge is described as the fire that can burn up all of one's karmic reactions. Karma, as we know, is a basic law of material nature through which the supreme authority and power of the Supreme Personality of Godhead is expressed. Karma means that one gets a reaction for any activity that is performed within the material world, in other words, it refers to the law of action and consequent reaction.

The Bhagavad Gita describes three types of karma, whereas 'karma' in these explanations is understood as action:

- **Karma:** Performance of those activities which have a reaction. This type of action generally allows the living entity to reach higher planets after leaving the present body or at least get another human body on earth. With the performance of karma, one is thereby entrapped in this vicious cycle of birth and death.
- **Vikarma:** This is the performance of illicit activities against the laws of nature. Each activity which ignores or opposes the Vedic injunctions or their basic activities can be considered to be in that category. These include torturing and killing of animals, theft, cheating, intoxication, illicit sex life, etc. Such activities are condemned and to be avoided at all costs.
- **Akarma:** The effect of the law of karma can only be avoided by transcendentalists who are engaged in akarma activities. Activities which don't cause karmic reactions are known as 'akarma'. This does not refer to material inertia by not doing anything. Purely transcendental

activities which are performed solely for the pleasure of Krishna are akarma. This type of activity qualifies us to reach the spiritual world after leaving our present body. This includes mantra meditation (or japa) of the Hare Krishna maha mantra, offering food to Krishna and honouring it as prasadam, congregational chanting of the Holy Name and performing devotional service by seeing everyone as part and parcel of Krishna.

- **Jnana-plava or the Boat of Knowledge:** The world that we live in is compared to a saltwater ocean with dangerous aquatic life that makes prolonged swimming difficult. As we can experience, the world that we live in has the three-fold miseries that we experience day in, day out.
  - miseries caused by one's body and mind (sickness, mental anxiety, fear, etc.)
  - miseries caused by other living entities (physical attack, theft and murder, etc.)
  - miseries caused by nature (earthquake, hurricane, tsunami, a pandemic like COVID, etc.)

Spiritual knowledge is the boat that protects us from the suffering of this oceanic world and carries one to the realm of unending and ever-expanding happiness in the spiritual realm. There is a beautiful verse in the *Srimad Bhagavatam* that describes how taking shelter of the Lotus Feet of Krishna (through authorized processes of chanting and sankirtan) helps cross this massive ocean with elan.

In the *Srimad Bhagavatam* (10.14.58), it is said: 'For those who have accepted the boat of the Lotus Feet of the Lord, who is the shelter of the cosmic manifestation and is famous as Murāri, the enemy of the Mura demon, the ocean of the material world is like the water contained in a calf's hoof print. Their goal is param padam, Vaikuṇṭha, the place where there are no material miseries, not the place where there is danger at every step.'

- **Jnana-dipa or the Lamp of Knowledge:** Walking in the dark is dangerous as we struggle to reach our desired destination. If we attempt to walk alone without taking help, we are likely to get a few powerful knocks on the way, in terms of getting hit somewhere or falling down or getting attacked by insects and animals not visible to the naked eye. As a result, we need to take the help of light, in the form of the spiritual master who helps us walk across the ocean of nescience. The spiritual master, or guru, should be considered to be directly the Supreme Lord because he gives transcendental knowledge for enlightenment. Consequently, it is said that for one who maintains the material conception that the spiritual master is an ordinary human being, everything is frustrated. His enlightenment and his Vedic studies and knowledge are like the bathing of an elephant. As you well know, the bathing of an elephant is considered useless, for an elephant cleanses itself by taking a full bath in the river, but then throws dust over its head and body as soon as it returns to the land.

FORTY-FOUR

The Key to Able Parenting

Human Quality: Maturity

A father and his three-year-old son walked out for Sunday shopping. They entered a grocery store first. Holding his child's hand, the father went around the store and filled his basket with items to be purchased. The shopkeeper carefully observed how the father-son duo were dealing with each other.

As the father was looking at various items in an aisle and making decisions in his mind whether to buy them or not, the son screamed, trying to drag his father outside the store.

The father held the boy carefully and said, 'Relax, Ram! Relax, Ram! Just a few more minutes, relax!' The boy stopped momentarily.

They went to another aisle, purchased some more items and the boy started shouting again. At this, the father repeated, 'Relax, Ram! Just a few more minutes; everything will be all right. Tolerate it for a few more minutes! Relax, Ram!'

This also happened at the third aisle; the son screamed so loudly that fellow customers looked at the father in disgust.

The father said again, 'Relax, Ram! Just the last few minutes. This is the last aisle. We are almost done.'

Then, as they reached the billing counter, as the items were being finalized and payment was in process, the boy shouted in his loudest voice. So much so that a customer approached the father, shared words of advice that his son better watch his behaviour and not spoil their Sunday morning.

Unfazed, the father repeated the same words, 'Relax, Ram! We are checking out now; we're making the payment. Everything will be all right. Relax, Ram!'

As the father-son duo exited the shop and proceeded towards their car, the shopkeeper keenly followed them.

Without disguising his amazement, he said to the father, 'Sir, I'm extremely impressed with the way you deal with your son, Ram.'

The father smiled.

'That was addressed in such a peaceful manner,' the shopkeeper added. 'You have so much patience. You have so much tolerance. You did not shout and scream at him even once. Your son is so fortunate to have a patient father like you.'

The father kept the grocery bag down, turned around, looked at the shopkeeper keenly and with a smile, said, 'Let me share the secret.'

'Sure, please tell me the secret to your patience,' the shopkeeper asked in excitement.

Chuckling, the father said, 'Actually, my name is Ram. My son's name is Shyam.'

The shopkeeper was shocked.

'As Shyam screams and throws tantrums,' the father added, 'I remind myself that I have to relax. That I need to be patient. That I must be tolerant. Ultimately, I am the adult and I must display maturity. It is my responsibility to behave myself and to demonstrate self-control.'

In relevance to such a situation in life, Krishna says in the Bhagavad Gita (5.23),

> *śaknotīhaiva yaḥ soḍhuṁ*
> *prāk śarīra-vimokṣaṇāt*
> *kāma-krodhodbhavaṁ vegaṁ*
> *sa yuktaḥ sa sukhī naraḥ*

In the human form of life, it's said that to be well-situated and happy, we have to tolerate the urges of the mind and the senses, especially the urges of lust and anger, till the moment of death. Provocations due to various circumstances will constantly bombard us. But maturity is to have ultimate patience and self-control and to not succumb to those provocations.

Patience is symptomized by:

- **Humility:** Acceptance of one's insignificance as a part and parcel of God makes us understand our insignificance in the manifestation of the world. When we don't think of ourselves as the doer, we remain humble. We are submissive to contribute to the larger universal order in a small way.
- **Faith:** We must accept the presence of a higher will when we understand that there is a higher power that drives

us all and that we are merely His instruments. Then, we are not agitated and humbly submit ourselves to play our parts and align ourselves with the larger universal order. We don't think of ourselves as the doer and hence remain patient.

- **Sincerity:** We must be willing to wait for the appropriate time. When we are sincere, we do not take things for granted or feel entitled to get instant results. We are committed to doing our duty sincerely with the hope and prayer that may God manifest results as per His desire and what is right for us.

- **Dedication:** Continuing to work with great absorption, dedication is about commitment to a certain cause or pursuit and the willingness to give it our 100 per cent no matter what comes in the way. It's about being mentally absorbed and wholeheartedly performing the duty as a service with the body, mind and soul invested in it.

Maturity is a state of being mentally and emotionally well-developed and therefore responsible. Maturity is also seen as the balance between courage and consideration. If a person expresses his feelings and convictions with courage balanced with consideration for the feelings and convictions of another person then one is mature, especially when issue is important to both parties.

Maturity in decision making is combination of:

- **Sukriti or Pious Credits:** Our state of mind is indeed a manifestation of our past sukriti. As Krishna says in the Gita, the state of mind that one was in at the time of death manifests in the succeeding birth. One key factor that contributes to our maturity is our past pious credits. From this, we can infer that we have an opportunity to shape the future by performing sukriti now to behave with greater maturity in the future.

- **Krpa or Blessings Due to Service:** Right from childhood, the habit of serving elders and taking their blessings is inculcated in us. The pure consciousness, filled with compassion and humility, with which we serve people helps us receive their blessings (krpa). This again is an important factor in us developing maturity.

- **Vivek or Discrimination Born Out of Experience:** As they say, experience is the best teacher. As we encounter different life situations, if we are able to remain patient, exercise self-restraint without getting agitated and apply ourselves with a clear mind, we discover different ways to deal with challenging situations. Yes, we may fail at times, but we learn with time. As we immerse ourselves in such experiences, we are able to sharpen our power of discrimination and develop our maturity quotient.

A combination of sukriti, krpa and vivek help us take mature decisions in life.

Therefore, we have the great opportunity to receive the great benedictions of the Supreme Lord, by demonstrating patience and maturity in decision making.

FORTY-FIVE

Power of Communication

Human Quality: Positive Thinking

In the Pandya kingdom, there lived a king who was superstitious. One night, while he was asleep, he had a bad dream. Terrified, he woke up from his sleep with a scream. The queen got disturbed, tried to enquire about it and comforted him. Without even responding to her, he rushed to the mirror and looked at his face. He opened his mouth and saw that everything was in place. Convinced that nothing had happened to him, he returned to the bed.

The queen enquired again, 'What happened? Please tell me.'

'I just had a bad dream. A very bad dream, I must say. Let me see the astrologer tomorrow.'

'But why the astrologer for this?' she asked.

'You don't understand. Please go back to sleep.'

The king gulped down a glass of water, prayed to God and went back to sleep.

The next morning, accompanied by his minister, he went to his astrologer and explained, 'I had a very bad dream last night.'

'I'm sorry to hear that,' the astrologer replied. 'What did you see?'

'In that dream,' the king continued, 'I saw that my teeth had fallen off.'

'Oh my God!' the astrologer exclaimed. 'It means that all your relatives will die, one after another before you.'

The king looked bewildered and was in denial. He decided to consult another astrologer. Taking the minister along, the king explained the dream to the astrologer. The response from the second astrologer was similar.

Confused, the king felt bogged down and sat in the chariot. Sensing discontentment in the king's mind, the minister politely offered help to the king.

'Can I help you here?' the minister asked.

Willing to hear him out, the king nodded in approval.

'Dear king, as far as the dream is concerned,' the minister affirmed, 'what they mean is that you are very lucky.'

'What?' the king looked at him in disbelief. 'What are you saying?'

'Yes, king,' the minister beamed. 'Your teeth will fall as you grow older. More importantly, when the astrologers concur that all your relatives will die before you, it just means that you will live longer. You are blessed by God. Long live the king! Congratulations.'

A wide smile filled the king's face. Blissful, he rewarded the minister.

The minister presented the same implication but in a positive manner. Therefore, things communicated positively have a positive impact.

In the *Srimad Bhagavatam* (10.13.3), there is a verse,

śṛṇuṣvāvahito rājann
api guhyaṁ vadāmi te
brūyuḥ snigdhasya śiṣyasya
guravo guhyam apy uta

The great masters, out of compassion for their students, speak positive truths of revealed scriptures to bring out the positivity within their hearts.

In our everyday life, we do try to remain positive, but we encounter situations that make us tilt towards negativity. Although it is not our intent entirely, the nature of the situation and the hardship that it entails sways us towards negativity. When the mind is not fully controlled, we get into the grip of external circumstances.

When faced with adversity, let us take help of the four-step formula to generate the fountain of positivity from the aquifer of our inner strength:

- **Awareness of the Gap between Expectation and Reality:**
  The root cause of sadness, it is said, is the gap between expectations and reality. As spirit soul, we are always in the search for happiness. That's the nature of the soul and there is no contesting there. However, because the soul is trapped within a material body, it tends to identify with the body. Now, the soul is subjected to material conditioning since time immemorial and due to material limitations, it is restricted in its capacity to enjoy. As a result, if our extent of desires surpasses the contours of material enjoyment, we develop sorrow. The first step to get out of this is to develop awareness of this gap that exists, that we may not always achieve what we desire.

When we are situated in this state of mind, we make progress and take the first step to remain positive

- **Affection of Family, Friends and Well-wishers Who Experience Our Pain and Empathize with Us:** As we battle adversity in life, we should understand that we are not alone in this battle. God has blessed us with a family of loving people who support us and are willing to help us get through the difficult phases of life. With this understanding, we should seek help, openly speak our minds to our near and dear ones and seek solace in that blanket of genuine love. As we get over this temporary phase of negativity, we can find positivity in the affectionate well-wishers and gradually elevate our mindset.

- **Analysis of Immediate and Remote Causes, and Further Realization That One Receives a Token Reaction of Past Actions Is a Step Further in the Direction to Positivity:** 'As you sow, so shall you reap' goes a famous saying. It's important to understand that every situation we go through in life is not by whim or a byproduct of randomness. It's a very calculated result of past actions. This is orchestrated through an inconceivable and invincible universal justice system known as the Law of Karma, as explained in the Bhagavad Gita. For one who is well-connected within, shows the right intent and puts the best foot forward at all times should understand that the enormity of misfortune could have been worse but the Supreme Lord, Krishna, is compassionate. He has shown only a glimpse of the overall pie, as a token reaction that is. When one develops this right understanding of situations, one feels grateful for the compassionate Lord, understands how fortunate one is to receive the mercy of Krishna and thereby cultivates positivity.

- **Absorption in a Bigger Cause Like Serving a Community and Empathizing with People to Resolve Their Pain Makes Our Adversity Look Insignificant:** When the mind is absorbed in activities of a higher nature and as we derive pleasure in enhancing the quality of life of others, our mind is comforted and becomes less affected by the condition of adversity. Further, sharing the difficult situations of people and striving to help them get through that phase can help us alleviate the mental depression and enable us to become more positive as a person.

Let us, therefore, adopt the steps mentioned above to embrace the spirit of positivity in terms of our attitude, outlook, perspective and speech, and, thus, create a positive transformation in our lives.

Acknowledgements

I wish to express my heartfelt gratitude to many wonderful souls who were part of the exciting journey of making this book happen, especially the wisdom and the lessons that are a part of every story.

My gratitude to His Divine Grace, Srila A.C. Bhaktivedanta Swami Prabhupada, the Founder Acharya of ISKCON, for publishing the essence of Vedic literatures, the Srimad Bhagavad Gita and the *Srimad Bhagawatam*, published by the Bhaktivedanta Book Trust International (BBT) in multiple languages, thus making the ancient Vedic wisdom accessible to all.

My gratitude to H.H. Radhanath Swami Maharaja for his personal guidance and training for nearly three decades and for facilitating my connection with Srila Prabhupada and ISKCON.

My heartfelt respects to H.H. Bhakti Rasamrita Swami Maharaja for introducing the concepts of *Bhagavad Gita* to me in my student days.

My gratitude to my father, Mr A.K. Sitaraman (Achyut Jagannatha Das), and my mother, Mrs Kalpakam Sitaraman (Sri Sachidevi Dasi), for nurturing my life with stories on spiritual wisdom and for being an excellent example of a stable and emotionally warm family, which created the foundation for absorbing the teachings of Vedic Sanatana Dharma.

I wish to offer my loving respects and feelings of gratitude to my senior leaders in ISKCON who have been the source of inspiration for me to live life following the teachings of *Srimad Bhagavatam* and share stories of spiritual lessons with the world:

H.H. Gopal Krishna Goswami Maharaja, H.H. Jayapataka Swami Maharaja, H.H. Bhakti Charu Swami Maharaja, H.H. Bhanu Swami Maharaja, H.H. Niranjana Swami Maharaja, H.H. Badrinarayana Swami Maharaja, H.H. Radha Govinda Goswami Maharaja, H.H. Sivarama Swami Maharaja, H.H. Bhakti Tirtha Swami Maharaja, H.H. Tamal Krishna Goswami Maharaja, H.H. Satsvarupa Das Goswami Maharaja, H.G. Bhurijana Prabhu, H.G. Shyamasundar Prabhu and many other disciples of Srila Prabhupada.

I acknowledge the wisdom I gained from many in the ashram, including Govinda Prabhu, Radha Gopinatha Prabhu, Shyamananda Prabhu, Sanatkumar Prabhu, Radheshyam Prabhu and Sankirtan Prabhu.

I have been highly inspired by the books, lectures and association of Shikshashtakam Prabhu, Gaurgopal Prabhu, Vrajavihari Prabhu, Chaitanya Charan Prabhu, Shubh Vilas Prabhu and Sutapa Prabhu, and acknowledge my gratitude to them for igniting many inspiring thoughts in me.

My special thanks to Suhail Mathur of The Book Bakers and Gurveen Chadha of Penguin Random House India for their patient and expert guidance, and intervention to craft the final version of the book.

My gratitude to the team of Ananda Caitanya Prabhu, Dr Sumanta Rudra, Gauranga Darshan Prabhu and the Bhaktivedanta Research Center (BRC) team for their support and help.

My gratitude to Rajesh Sridhar for his diligent work on every aspect of the book taking its final shape. Special thanks to Vinay Raniga and Vrushali Potnis Damle for their help with proofreading and editing.